GUIGO II

THE LADDER OF MONKS
and
TWELVE MEDITATIONS

CISTERCIAN STUDIES SERIES: NUMBER FORTY-EIGHT

THE LADDER OF MONKS
A Letter on the Contemplative Life

and

TWELVE MEDITATIONS

by

GUIGO II

Translated, with an Introduction by
Edmund Colledge, OSA
and James Walsh, SJ

CISTERCIAN PUBLICATIONS
Kalamazoo, Michigan — Spencer, Massachusetts

The work of Cistercian Publications is made possible in
part by support from Western Michigan University to
the Institute of Cistercian Studies.

Published by arrangement with Doubleday & Company, Inc.

Library of Congress Cataloguing in Publication Data

Guigo II, d. 1188.
   The ladder of monks.

   Translation of Scala claustralium and Meditationes.
   1. Spiritual life–Catholic authors. 2. Meditations. I.
   Guigo II, d. 1188. Meditationes. English. 1978. II. Colledge,
   Edmund. III. Walsh, James, 1920– IV. Title.
   BX2349.G8513   242'.1

   Doubleday edition:
   Library of Congress Catalog Card Number 77-11230
   ISBN 0-385-13596-3

   Cistercian Publications edition:
   Library of Congress Catalog Card Number 81-30
   ISBN 0-87907-748-4 & 848-0 (hc)

Typeset by Humble Hills Graphics
Printed in the United States of America

TABLE OF CONTENTS

GUIGO II

THE LADDER OF MONKS
and
TWELVE MEDITATIONS

§

INTRODUCTION

1

INTRODUCTION

The Life and Writings of Guigo II

DOM ANDRÉ WILMART wrote of the early Carthusians: 'These men, austere and discreet, founded their hermitages so that they could live in silence among the shadows, occupied in meditating upon eternal truths. We do not expect self-revelation from them.'[1] This is especially true of Guigo, the ninth prior of the mother house, the Grande Chartreuse. What little can be learned of his life is set out in orderly fashion by Wilmart;[2] and since he wrote, nothing has been added to our knowledge.

He appears as witness to an agreement made in 1173 between his house and the near-by abbey of Chalais, and he is there called 'monk and procurator'. In that year or the next, according to Le Couteulx, he was made prior;[3] and he is so styled in two papal bulls of 1176 and 1177. About the year 1180, when Henry II of England asked for his successor as procurator, Hugh, the future bishop of Lincoln and canonized saint, to be sent to England to the new Carthusian foundation at Witham, Guigo unsuccessfully opposed this request, saying that he looked to Hugh as his chief support in his old age. In 1180 Guigo was replaced as prior, but he is mentioned in the chronicles of the house in 1185 as 'former prior'. Most recent authorities agree that he died in 1188:[4] Le Couteulx would date his death as c. 1193, but this is only because he accepted the false ascription to Guigo of Adam the Carthusian's *Fourfold Exercise,* the dedicatory epistle of which shows that it must have been composed in the years after the general chapter of 1186-87, when its author discussed the form it should take with Bovo, the prior of Witham, to whom the work is addressed.

Le Couteulx tells us that after his resignation as prior, Guigo spent his remaining years in solitude;[5] and elsewhere he states as his own opinion and that of earlier historians of the Order that the chronicle of the house kept during the rule of the succeeding prior refers to Guigo when it tells of 'A certain monk, outstanding for his most holy life and obedience', at whose grave so many miracles of healing were performed that the concourse of pilgrims seeking favors was wholly disrupting the solitude and the good conduct of the Grande Chartreuse, until the prior went to where the monk was buried, and commanded him in the name of the holy obedience which he had so perfectly followed in life to cease his intercession in Heaven for such miracles.[6] The story can be paralleled—Bernard's successor laid the same prohibition on him, the sainted Augustinian dead at Lecetto outside Siena were once put under the same obedience, and for the same reason[7]—but it shows that Guigo must have enjoyed after his death among the brethren a quite singular reputation for sanctity.

For the rest, if we want to know what kind of man Guigo was, we can only rely on suppositions drawn from the nature of his religious vocation and the offices he held, as well as on the evidence of his writings; and here we meet some difficulty, because by far the greater number of the manuscripts containing copies of the three works he may have written, the *Ladder of Monks,* the twelve *Meditations* and the separate Meditation on the *Magnificat,* either attribute them to other men or are silent about their authorship. This is a constant problem in the study of medieval literature. Few writers, even of secular literature, could hope for any financial reward, once a first copy had been issued for publication or presented to a patron, so that even now there are many classics of the Middle Ages whose authors we cannot name.

Often there were positive reasons for this anonymity: Controversial writers in such fields as theology and politics sometimes found it prudent not to put their names to their work. The Carthusians from their earliest days followed this general policy, though for different reasons. They deplored anything that would interrupt their silence and seclusion, and they discouraged their members from seeking, for themselves or for other brethren, any outward marks of distinction, whether of learning or of sanctity. But all such anonymous publications opened the way to another source of confusion, the attribution to one man, usually a famous name from times past, of another's work. Many such false ascriptions were made by later scribe-editors in good faith: they might be guided by marked similarities to the content or style of some classic, similarities more common in an age when dependence upon authority was reckoned a literary virtue; or they might be misled by the appearance in a volume, largely containing the genuine writings of some author, of other pieces not stated to be not from his pen. Sometimes, however, a scribe's motives were less creditable: if a large volume of 'Augustine' or 'Bernard' would fetch more from an unsuspecting purchaser than a small one, many saw little harm in borrowing from other writers to fill out such volumes.

Guigo's writings certainly suffered this fate, largely, we suspect, because neither he nor the Grande Chartreuse showed any concern for his personal reputation as a spiritual writer. The great number of manuscripts of the *Ladder* identified by Wilmart, and those which have since been found, reveal that fifty-nine attribute it to Bernard, sixteen to Augustine, three to 'Guido' (a common error for 'Guigo', so that these, like the manuscript of the *Meditations* so attributed, may be reckoned as correctly described), two each to Bonaventura and 'Guigo', one each to Anselm, 'Goffredus' and 'Frater P'.

Only seven complete manuscripts of the *Meditations*[8] are known: four of these are ascribed to Bernard, one to 'Hugo, prior of Chartreuse' (Wilmart satisfactorily showed that this, too, counts as a true attribution), one to 'Guido, prior to the Chartreuse' and one is unattributed. Three of the five manuscripts of the meditation on the *Magnificat* which have been consulted say that it is by Bernard, two are unattributed.[9]

The Scala Claustralium

HISTORY AND MANUSCRIPT TRADITION

We must be guided by the contents of each work, and by its manuscript tradition, in deciding whether the attribution to Guigo is genuine, and whether we can safely disregard other attributions.

To deal first with the *Ladder*, it will be seen, when its sources are presently discussed, that it draws on numerous writers of the second half of the twelfth century, which rules out Augustine as a possible author. As regards the manuscript tradition, as long ago as 1924 Wilmart published two articles[10] in which he assessed some Carthusian contributions to spiritual writing in the twelfth and thirteenth centuries; and in 1932 these were reproduced as Chapter XIV of his *Auteurs spirituels,* with additional material embodying the results of his further investigations into the problems presented by these diverse attributions of the *Ladder* and the confusion between the persons and the writings of the fifth prior of the Grande Chartreuse, Guigo I, author of the *Consuetudines,* and of Guigo II.

In the Migne Augustine, the work is given the title *Ladder of Paradise.*[11] The text ascribed to Bernard is called *Ladder for Monks, or a Treatise on Methods of Praying;*[12] and in many manuscripts its title is *A Treatise on Four Steps of the Spiritual Life* or *A Treatise on Spiritual Exercise.* Both printed texts show it to be a carefully considered and constructed treatise; but Wilmart's assessment of the value of the early manuscripts satisfied him that those who had preserved the archetype with least subsequent editorial work had retained a prologue and an epilogue, lost in most surviving copies, showing that this treatise was couched in the form of a letter, addressed by Guigo to his brother in religion Gervase.

Prologue, epilogue and attribution are lost in the text in Migne printed among the works of Augustine; and though the other, appearing among Bernard's *spuria,* retains them, both texts reflect a tradition established only three centuries after the work was first composed, when it was re-edited and given wide publication under the influence of the *Devotio Moderna.* Wilmart noted that the treatise was in the hands of Cardinal Pierre d'Ailly before the Council of Constance in 1414. D'Ailly made his own recension of Guigo's work; and in 1482 this recension was published by the Brethren of the Common Life. In this, Bernard is called the author, and the title is *On Four Steps.* But a very similar text with, however, attribution to Augustine and titled *Ladder of Paradise,* had appeared in Milan in 1475; and Wilmart considered that the tradition which such texts represent derives from a type of manuscript in many respects notably deficient.

It was also Wilmart's opinion that the medieval attribution to Bernard, which is not implausible since the author was full of Bernard's teaching and owed several of his ideas to him, might still in the twentieth century have been accepted, had not Horstius in 1641 reported his discovery of a manuscript of the authentic tradition, attributing the work to 'Guigo', with no other identification. When Mabillon re-edited Bernard's works he did not reject this new theory, though expressing certain reservations.[13] He repeated Horstius's statement about the manuscript from which this information was derived, that it formerly belonged to the Cologne Charterhouse and that it named the author as Guigo the Carthusian, who, Mabillon pointed out, must be either the fifth or the ninth prior of the Grande Chartreuse. Unfortunately, Mabillon added to the confusion surrounding 'Guigo' by

attributing to him the treatise, addressed to the prior and
Charterhouse of Witham, *The Fourfold Exercise of the Cell,*
which has in recent times been definitely restored to its
rightful author, Adam of Dryburgh, who began his religious
life as a canon of Premontré, but later became a Carthusian.[14]
The scholars responsible for the notices of Guigo I and
Guigo II in the *Histoire Littéraire*[15] rightly concluded that
only Guigo II could have written the *Scala;* but, though they
were followed in this by the historian of the Carthusian order,
Le Couteulx, he drew wrong conclusions about the dates of
Guigo's career, through accepting the false ascription to him
of the *Fourfold Exercise.*

In 1932 Wilmart was promising a new critical text of the
Ladder. The latter years of his life were spent working in
England; and among unpublished papers of his, now preserved
at Quarr Abbey, a recension was found, evidently made as
part of the apparatus for his Guigo articles. It was based upon
most of the manuscripts of his 'Group I', to be described
below with his other groupings; but he had used for his text
the Vatican Barberini manuscript, Va, and it would seem that
only after such a recension had been prepared did he discover
the manuscript used by Horstius and Mabillon, the surviving
Darmstadt manuscript, Da, also of Group I. It was perhaps an
understandable reluctance to revise his recension which led
him to disprize this Darmstadt codex. Before the present
editors had access to his unpublished papers, they had, however, collated those manuscripts that he had indicated in
Auteurs spirituels as representing the authentic tradition, and
had already decided that Da, on grounds of attribution,
integrity of text and regular superiority of readings, is the best
manuscript of Group I. Accordingly, the translation in this
edition is based on it.

Wilmart's unpublished notes show that in the course of his
enquiries he had identified ninety-three manuscript copies of
the *Ladder,* ranging in date from the two in the Bibliothèque
Nationale (Pa 1, Pa 2) and the Barberini manuscript in the

Biblioteca Vaticana (Va), which are of the thirteenth century, to that in the Bibliothèque Royale in Brussels, which is dated 1545. Wilmart successfully grouped all these, and showed how all but his Group I could safely be ignored, an achievement which has greatly facilitated the work of his successors.

Group I contains the whole text as Guigo wrote it, with the prologue, giving in some cases the name of the Gervase, to whom the treatise was addressed, Guigo's own name and the epilogue, except for the manuscripts at Prague (Pr), which omits the entire epilogue, and that at Utrecht (Ut), which omits its last sentence.

Group II lacks the prologue; Group III both prologue and epilogue; and Group IV not only follows III in this, but undertakes a fundamental rearrangement of the body of the text. The general nature of this recension is described elsewhere, in dealing with the Middle English translation of the *Ladder,* which was made from a Latin text of this type. Wilmart was able further to subdivide the copies of this group into five categories, according to the point at which they break off, although these terminations are frequently improved upon and elaborated by individual scribes. IV(a) ends with '*ut haec et alia impedimenta auferat a nobis*' (11. 495-97), IV(b) with '*iterum curabit et sanabit nos*' (11. 492-93), IV(c) with '*quanto a primo gradu remotior*' 437-38), IV(d) with '*eius dulcedine trahebar invitus*' (1. 312), IV(e) with '*delicatus est sponsus iste, nobilis est*' (1. 302). It is noteworthy that all identifiable manuscripts of IV(c) are German in origin, all of IV(d) and IV(e) that are identifiable originate in England.

Recent enquiries have produced further manuscripts. Wilmart knew five at Prague, of which one belongs to Guigo I, and indicated the existence of nine others. Four are at Uppsala: three, all attributed to Augustine, belong to Group III, one, unattributed, to Group IV(a) and all four are of the fifteenth century. York Minster possesses one, written c. 1400, unattributed, of Group IV(a), Stockholm has one, fifteenth century, attributed to Bernard. On December 7, 1964, at a Sotheby's sale a German, fifteenth-century manuscript containing two texts of the *Ladder,* both of Group IV, was sold to Maggs. Washington has one, written c. 1500 in an Italian humanist hand, also of Group IV, but remarkable for a long interpolation in what, in the original text, is Chapter XV, where, before the passage beginning '*Sed o Deus bone, suavis et mitis . . .* ', a later editor has introduced some seven hundred words of digression, suggested by what immediately precedes them in Guigo's text, '*et vere despexisti me, et non solum sermones meas sed meipsum projecisti retrorsum et ambulasti post concupiscentias tuas*', upon the miserable frailties and shortcomings of human nature, and man's unkindness toward God. Such an interpolation has not been found in any other manuscript and would seem to be of recent composition.

Faced with this plethora of manuscripts, but helped by Wilmart's work on them, the present editors decided that to collate them all would be unrewarding and superfluous, the more so as it is clear that there must still be unidentified copies that will appear from time to time. Instead, attention was confined to Group I, to which were added Pa 1 and Pa 2, manuscripts of Group II which none the less are very early and often contain valuable variants. Unfortunately, no trace has yet been found of another potentially important text, that was once contained in the Phillips collection, but sold in 1910, in the hands of a Lille bookseller before 1914, and now untraceable.[16] According to the sale catalogue, the text of the *Ladder,* which it contained, was entitled *S. Bernardi Scala claustralium,* which suggests that it belonged to Groups II or III; but, like Da, it was a fifteenth-century copy made in the Cologne Charterhouse, and so might have given readings worthy of consideration. With the evidence at their disposal, however, the editors have had no hesitation in basing their work on Da: and a subsequent comparison of their text with Wilmart's provisional edition shows that where he and Da conflict, Da usually has the better reading. Da seems to be derived, in Group I, from an older copy singularly free from error and close to the archetype; and even its unique title, which Wilmart dismisses as 'factitious', is as likely to be the sole survivor of such a good copy as to represent the work of an intelligent editor of a later epoch. Wilmart may have thought that the literary form of the treatise was not sufficiently epistolary in style to warrant Da's title as authentic. There is, however, more than one indication in the course of the work that the author considered himself to be throughout writing a letter. While evaluating scores of manuscripts that carry no reference either to the writer or the recipient, Wilmart may well have been influenced by these later developments, with their stress on the strong didactic elements at the expense of Guigo's original plan, so that he tended to overlook that it is precisely what the Da title calls it, a letter on the structure of the contemplative life.

The Ladder of Monks

DOCTRINE AND SOURCES

The prologue is addressed to a 'Brother Gervase', and it tells us that although the two men were at one time closely associated, they are now apart, even though they still write to each other.

We may think that Wilmart was too ready to accept the identification of the recipient with Gervase, third prior of Mont-Dieu, which is a mere supposition: and even if we do accept this, it does not follow that the *Scala* was composed before 1159, the putative date for the end of Gervase's priorate, since it is disputed whether his office ended with his death or resignation.

What is clear is that the Gervase addressed stood to the author in a special relationship. Guigo calls himself a beginner and a theoretician in that spiritual science of which Gervase is a master, and he asks for the other's judgment on his book. This protestation of ignorance, as the whole of the *Ladder* shows, does not correspond with the facts; but these demonstrations of humility, and of due reverence for one's seniors and former teachers, are commonplace in such writings. Gervase, he says, was indeed responsible for settling him in his present way of life. We cannot say whether the Scriptural imagery he here employs means that it was Gervase who first attracted him out of the world into religion, or rather that Gervase was the guide for the first steps of a still-untutored religious in the interior life.

But the language which Guigo uses, 'the young tree extracted from the bondage of Pharaoh' (not itself a very happy union of two separate Old Testament texts) 'set in its place amongst the ordered rows', reveals at once two sources of such imagery already dear to Guigo, the Book of Exodus and the Canticles. He quotes both frequently in the *Meditations,* and will do so several times again in the *Ladder.* There is nothing remarkable in this, a fondness, especially for the imagery and the spiritual senses of Canticles, to be observed among all his contemporaries, whether Carthusians, Cluniacs, Premonstratensians or Cistercians. Like his predecessor, Guigo I and their founder Bruno, Guigo has little or nothing to say that betrays a specifically Carthusian profession. Toward the close of the Middle Ages we may find the Carthusians somewhat self-conscious in their stress upon their uniquely solitary character; but they are then only saying that they had conserved what the other reforming monastic movements of the eleventh and twelfth centuries had also aimed at, but had, in some measure, since lost. In their beginnings they all aspired to a cenobitic solitude, exterior as well as interior.

The spirituality that Guigo teaches fits exactly the name, invented by Abbot Cuthbert Butler and universally accepted: it is that 'Western mysticism', the first professional exponent of which is Augustine, and which still flourished, faithful to its original sources and equal to the task of absorbing such extraneous influences as the Dionysian canon, on the very eve of the dissolution of the religious houses where it was practiced. It is in no way surprising that the *Ladder* should have been so variously ascribed, to Augustine, Bernard, Anselm and even Bonaventura; and perhaps the most significant tribute to it, and the clearest proof that it reflects faithfully the contemplative traditions of the West, is the importance attached to it by the latest of the pre-Reformation *devoti,* the Brethren of the Common Life.

But this Western spirituality, we must remember, had inherited the genesis of its teachings on the contemplative life from yet older sources. Dom Jean Leclercq has written '[Western contemplatives] had collected, preserved, experimented with that which had been the common doctrine of the ancient Eastern Church concerning hesychasm, and had then given it expression in language drawn from Biblical poetry and adapted to the usage of Western civilization in the twelfth century, which appears as a very great epoch in the history of mediaeval spirituality because it gave fresh impetus to what it had so faithfully conserved'.[17] And Fr. Hausherr has said of this doctrine of hesychasm, *otia monastica,* of the necessity for the contemplative of renunciation of worldly preoccupations, that 'St. Basil says that the ascetic life has one goal alone, the safety of the soul, and the soul will be saved through love; so that the soul seeks no other wisdom, knows no other duty than to recognize and to accept that form of life which will lead it most surely to the most supreme love'.[18] For twelfth-century monks as for all other hesychasts, this is contemplative union, which is the real matter of the *Ladder.*

Guigo in his Prologue says that the work consists of 'my thoughts on the spiritual exercises proper to cloistered monks', for whom the primacy of the contemplative over the active life is the initial condition of their vocation. This is

the counsel that Bruno had given to his friend Raoul de
Verde: much as Raoul's archbishop may need his help and
advice in the world, there are greater claims upon his love,
the claims of a God who has already shown Himself as
the one good worthy of our love;[19] and a contemporary of
Bernard, the Cistercian Galland of Regny, writes that if
cloistered monks call happy those, vowed to different forms
of obedience, whom they see taking their part in the life of
the world, and if they long also to live so, they are preferring
the evil to the good, or, at least, the lesser to the greater
good. To live the enclosed and contemplative life, chastely
and in common, is the beginning of the life of the world to
come, it is the life of the angels; it is no perishable bread that
is labored for, but fruits that will endure for ever. And then
Galland uses Paul's words, as Guigo will allude to them in
Chapter XI of the *Ladder:* The soul is espoused as a chaste
virgin, and shall know no husband but Christ.[20]

Chapter 2 is called in Da (the titles in which have been
reproduced even though they are not found in all other
manuscripts) 'The Four Rungs of the Ladder'; and Guigo
comes at once to the heart of his treatise. His spiritual exercises are stages, steps, rungs, leading the devout soul up
toward union with God, and he names them in ascending
order.

This analogy for man's interior ascent to God of a ladder
or stairway is of great antiquity.[21] It originates in the account
in Genesis, to which Guigo alludes, of Jacob's vision, and for
early Christians it was reinforced by our Lord's prophecy to
the Apostles in St. John Chapter 1. In the mid-third century
Origen used the analogy when he established the sequence
that became standard for later writers upon progress in contemplation. For him the ladder has three upward grades: the
step of purgation; the second for proficients, that of illu-
mination; and the third, the step of unitive prayer, which is
for the perfect. This is the scheme followed some three centuries later by Dionysius, and it is their scheme that informs

the *Ladder*. In Guigo's own age many writers had used the theme for their own ends. Bruno, for example, finds the soul's ascent typified by the gradual psalms, which signify for him a progress through fifteen stages of blessedness.[22] Richard of St. Victor uses it for the title of two short works, *The Stages of Love* and *The Four Stages of Impetuous Love*.[23] From our point of view, the first of these is something of a misnomer: though Richard does speak of the need for the soul's purgation, the treatise deals with the soul's total absorption in love, which he compares with Paul's rapture, when it has attained to unitive prayer. *The Four Stages* was itself to become a classic, constantly quoted (it supplies Rolle, for instance, with doctrine and vocabulary), and it does treat of four ascending degrees, 'wounding love', 'languishing love', 'dissolving love' and 'consuming love', but here too we can see that Richard is not concerned, as in other of his works, with the psychology of prayer, but is wholly occupied by the phenomena of mystical union, and Guigo's use of the ladder-analogy is not inspired by Richard's, but by the tradition established with Origen.

Guigo discerns four ascending steps, which he calls 'reading', 'meditation', 'prayer' and 'contemplation'; and he goes on to define his terms. This is in itself remarkable, for we shall find that long after Guigo, indeed, to the end of the medieval period, many authoritative writers on the spiritual life confuse their readers by suing such terms, 'meditation' and 'contemplation' in particular, interchangeably and imprecisely. Bernard, before Guigo, had seen the necessity for precision, when, in *De consideratione* II.2, he had written: 'I do not wish everything to be understood by "consideration" which "contemplation" implies. Contemplation gives us certainty about facts, consideration enquires what the facts are. Contemplation can define . . . , but consideration is an intense application of the mind to enquire, or the intention of the mind as it seeks for truth.'[24]

We can be sure that Guigo knew this definition, but he

goes beyond it in the practicality of his own. Like Bernard's 'consideration', his two first steps are carefully separated from 'contemplation', and concern the inquiring mind; but the first, reading, tells where the mind must inquire, in the Scriptures. (Though *scriptura* was often used in its wider sense to include, for example, the Fathers and commentators, in all that Guigo says to exemplify these processes, he is wholly occupied with the Bible alone.) This places the examination on a firmer footing than that which we find, for example, in Hugh of St. Victor's *Homily I on Ecclesiastes*, though this, undoubtedly, was one of the models that Guigo used. Hugh teaches that the rational soul has three modes of vision, *cogitatio, meditatio, contemplatio* (thinking, meditating, contemplating); but all that he has to say of 'thinking' is that it is 'a fleeting notion of a thing, prompted either by the senses or the memory'.[25]

In the brief Chapter 3, 'The Functions of These Degrees', Guigo clarifies his distinction by application and example. The soul's aim is the sweetness of a life that is blessed; and to attain this, reading seeks, meditation perceives, prayer asks and contemplation tastes. Here he is adapting to his own purposes Bernard's remark in *De consideratione:* 'That truth which no word explains is sought by consideration, is asked for by prayer, and may it be merited by the soul's life, attained by its purity';[26] and he is doubtless recalling where Hugh says, in *Homily I on Ecclesiastes,* that what meditation seeks contemplation possesses.[27] In exemplifying this, Guigo introduces the analogy he had already explored in Meditation X; reading puts food whole into the mouth, meditation chews on it, prayer extracts its flavor, and contemplation tastes its sweetness. One of the first begetters of this analogy, which Guigo's Cistercian contemporaries are at constant pains to emphasize, is Augustine, in *De quantitate animae* 70, where he writes that the soul nourishes itself as the body does: seeking strength 'it draws it together and keeps it together, not allowing it to flow or melt away: it distributes nourishment proportionately to each member'.[28]

Chapter 4, 'The Function of Reading', introduces the text to which Guigo intends to apply the processes he has described, Matthew 5:8, 'Blessed are the pure in heart, for they shall see God'. This is not merely for the sake of demonstration. This text, its affirmation and its promise, will supply the constant connecting theme of the rest of the treatise, and Guigo says of it at once that it is of great sweetness, 'filled with many senses to feed the soul'. We may compare what pseudo-Bede says of the same text, that those 'who seek God alone, having no bitterness in them, forsaking all vanities and contemplating God with unfeigned love, possess the spirit of understanding, for to their gaze is revealed the treasure-house of wisdom'.[29]

Guigo begins Chapter 5, 'The Function of Meditation', with an entirely traditional demonstration of method.[30] In turn, the affirmation, 'Blessed are the pure in heart', and the promise, 'For they shall see God', are illuminated by adducing relevant Old Testament quotations to point and show their meaning; and this method is compared first with the chewing of the grape to extract its juice, then with the striking of a spark to kindle fire. This second analogy is a commonplace, but when Guigo continues that the flames so kindled must be fanned, he may be recalling Hugh of St. Victor's use of it, when he compares the ascending modes of comprehension with the fire we first see as flames and smoke, then as fire with either flames or smoke, then finally, as fire alone.[31] Then, introducing another metaphor, Guigo compares these first intimations of sweetness with the sweet odor from a broken box of ointment. For this metaphor he may be indebted to William of St. Thierry's *Second Exposition on the Canticles,* where he talks of the *altitudo contemplationis* (height of contemplation) that will comprehend and surpass all the spiritual senses, and be signified by 'some faint murmur of your voice, some little taste of your sweetness, some scent of your perfumes'.[32] The soul is so consumed by

longing; and the more it searches, the more it thirsts. This
idea, already hinted at in Meditation XI, is a commonplace:
Guigo may have known it in Richard of St. Victor's *Four
Stages of Impetuous Love,* or in one of its archetypal pre-
sentations, in Augustine's *Enarratio in Ps. 41.*[33] In this meditation there is no spiritual attainment, 'unless it be given from
above', because such meditation is merely an intellectual
process, which good and bad can exercise, that was practiced
by the pagan philosophers, who had the power to recognize
a highest good that they had not the grace to understand.
Here Guigo demonstrates very clearly his adherence to the
traditional anti-intellectualism of mystical theology, which
had been voiced in the Western Church for centuries before
the Dionysius canon was known there.[34] In his last point in
this chapter, where the contrast between a merely intellectual recognition of God and the inward experience of Him
which through grace is compared with the difference between
the office of baptizing, entrusted by God to many, and the
remission of sins by baptism, reserved to God alone, Guigo
seems to be recalling Hugh of St. Victor's *De sacramento
baptismi,* where he ends such a discussion by quoting an un-
named pope: 'Who baptizes a man does not judge him, but
assists in administering the grace of baptism, which is of the
Spirit of God.'[35]

This theme is pursued in Chapter 6, 'The Function of
Prayer'. Recognition of the incapacity of the intellect to
attain to what the soul longs for brings to it a deeper
humility. Reading and meditation have brought knowledge
of God, but 'only a little'; and it is no mere intellectual ap-
prehension that the soul desires, but to see Him as He is.
Inevitably, Guigo utters these longings in the words of the
Psalmist, and he is very close to the thought and the language
employed by William of St. Thierry, when, for example, in
the seventh of his *Meditative Prayers,* alluding to a different
passage from the Psalm, he writes: 'It is your face I seek, and
I implore you not to turn it from me; but, till I see it, teach

me, O everlasting Wisdom, by the light of your countenance, what is the meaning of this "face to face".'[36] William, in *De contemplando Deo,* Chapter 1, expresses in an extended and more rhetorical form the point made here by Guigo's simple quotation again of 'except by the pure of heart': The soul will come to recognize how rash, how presumptuous, how disordered, how overweening, how alien to the rule taught by divine truth and wisdom is any longing of an impure heart to see God.[37] (This entire passage in William is a happy example of the 'burning words', the 'spells' by which the soul seeks to draw its spouse of which Guigo speaks at the beginning of his next chapter.) But meditation upon this vision has merely increased the longing for it: The soul has now been fed upon the Scriptures, and cannot be any longer satisfied with any exterior knowledge; Scripture has shown that it has an interior, hidden meaning, and this the soul asks for, not as in any way merited, but as a grace and a free gift. All it can do is confess its unworthiness, and ask for what Guigo, using the romantic symbol frequent in his age,[38] calls the *arrha,* the pledge, the bridegroom's first betrothal gift, 'one drop of heavenly rain with which to refresh my thirst'.

Then he turns, in Chapter 7, 'The Effects of Contemplation', from this consideration of the soul's inadequacies to write of the first intimations of God's co-operation in this work of prayer. The soul by its prayers has inflamed its own desires (Guigo seems here to be quoting Gregory, 'When the mind longs in prayer to see the face of its creator, it is inflamed with divine desires'),[39] and God, understanding not merely its halting words but their intention, interrupts them to give the soul that pledge of His love for which it is asking. This we may compare with what William of St. Thierry writes, in *De natura et dignitate amoris* IV 10, of how the soul, still laboring under the burden of its longings, will suddenly begin to be revived and illumined by frequent and unexpected manifestations of God *(frequentes et improvisae theophaniae)* and glimpses of the glories of the saints.[40] The consolations which the soul now receives Guigo describes in traditional, biblical terms: it is 'sprinkled with sweet, heavenly dew', it is 'anointed with most precious perfumes', and so, refreshed and restored, it forgets all earthly things, it dies to itself and so receives new life. The chapter ends with an observation drawn from human psychology: Just as the body's functions can sometimes subdue and enslave the soul (Augustine had remarked on this in his Sermon 156),[41] now the soul, so consoled, can quell every opposition of the flesh.

Chapters 8, 'The Signs of the Coming of Grace', and 9, 'How Grace Is Hidden', are probably inspired by Hugh of St. Victor's *De arrha animae,* toward the end of which comes a passage on sighs and tears as consolations and tokens of grace,[42] which was thereafter constantly to be copied, alluded to and elaborated in affective writings (the same idea is expressed by William of St. Thierry, in his *Meditative Prayers,* no. 4).[43] Many others follow Guigo in developing the idea of a *ludus amoris* (game of love), the spouse's recurrent visiting of the soul and then his withdrawal. This is knowledge hidden from those who have not experienced it: only those who have known this 'game of love' can understand how God can leave the soul, to be more ardently longed for, and yet can remain with it in unbroken union.

The theme is continued in Chapter 10, 'How, When Grace Is Hidden for a Time, It Works in Us for Good'. The bride of the spouse, the soul, is not to fear or despair when it is made the sport of this 'game of love': There is profit in God's withdrawing, just as in His coming. In this way the soul is put on its guard against pride and complacency. 'He comes to you, and then He goes away again': these are also Hugh's words, in *De arca Noe morali* IV 4, where he writes: 'But what is this? He seeks when He is not sought, when He is not called He comes, but when He is sought, He turns aside, and when He is called He flees . . . But He calls us to His own country, for this land of ours is no fit dwelling-place for such a love.'[44] Guigo adopts this idea also: the soul must be put on its guard lest it despise its brethren, lest it attribute what is of grace to its own natural powers, lest it mistake earth for heaven. The soul must lift up its heart 'to where I am at the right hand of God the Father'. Plainly, this refers us back to the earlier chapters, to the vision of God, granted in contemplation, which is beyond mere intellect; and here Guigo may be recalling Augustine's Sermon 243, where he collates St. Luke 8:43–46, 'Someone has touched me', with St. John 20:17, 'Do not touch me, for I have not yet ascended to my Father', and says that those who know that Christ is seated at His Father's right hand have touched Him, that those who think Him a man and no more have not yet enjoyed the fruits of the Resurrection.[45]

At the end of Chapter 11, 'How Much the Soul Must Be on Its Guard . . . ' , Guigo apologizes for what Gervase may regard as a digression, which, he explains, he has been constrained to make out of 'the abundance and the sweetness of my material'. In it he explores further the ideas already suggested by the comparison of God's first inpourings of grace with the bridegroom's betrothal gift. Here the soul, in the absence of such consolations, is compared with the betrothed virgin waiting for the bridegroom's return and for her wedding day. Even in his absence he keeps jealous watch over her, and if she is not to be rejected by him, who is so nobly born and rich and fair, she must preserve all a virgin's qualities. In this chapter Guigo is using the analogy, fleetingly suggested several times in the *Meditations,* between the soul's infidelity to God and adultery, which has its origins in the Old Testament in Hosea and elsewhere, but which, from the early twelfth century onward in Western Europe, owes much of its force to the similarities it possessed to the ideas and forms of the secular literature of courtly love.

The medieval editors of the *Ladder* call Chapter 12 a 'recapitulation', but in fact it proffers fresh ideas. The reader will have perceived that there is a causal as well as a temporal sequence in these four stages of spiritual progress, and Guigo

refers this causal connection to human psychology. In
reading we exercise the senses, and meditation refers what is
perceived by the senses to the intellect. In prayer we express
our emotional reactions to our intellectual evaluations, and
contemplation grants us, as God's response to our petitions, a
mode of perception and feeling in which our faculties are
transcended. And this causal connection is also shown in the
soul's stages of progress. The beginner, reading, will advance
by meditation to proficiency, by prayer to devotion, and in
contemplation to blessedness.

Chapter 13, 'How These Degrees Are Linked to One
Another', pursues this new theme. The causal connection
between the stages of progress is so essential that each one
must lead to the next. Otherwise we shall be wasting our time
and drifting into mere sentimentality. It is true that we can
do nothing without God (Guigo's Latin here seems to echo
the Collect for the First Sunday after Pentecost, *et quia sine
te nihil potest mortalis infirmitas*—and since without you
mortal weakness can do nothing), but it is just as true that
God demands our willing co-operation. Guigo here quotes
Paul, and the reminiscences of Augustine are plain to see.
Then, by way of *exemplum*, he ends the chapter with a
'mystical' interpretation of the story of the Samaritan woman
as a type of contemplative prayer. To us this may seem
arbitrary and forced, his gloss on 'Call your husband' in
particular; but there would be no place here for any consideration of the literal sense, the wonderful example the story
gives of a heart burdened with sin being moved to contrition,
and to Guigo's contemporaries his application would seem
entirely permissible.

Chapter 14, 'Some Conclusions from What Has Been Said',
is much more a recapitulation of what has gone before. Guigo
pursues the idea of the uselessness of one stage without the
others, and later he repeats that they are so linked that to
separate them is to destroy their efficacy. The metaphor used
here, as several times before, that of the chain the links of

which cannot function except in correlation, has less force for us than for any medieval reader, who would recognize at once that Guigo is appealing to the concept of the 'chain of being', of the dependence of every form of life, through higher forms, upon the first link of the chain, upon the source of all being, the Creator. But in regarding this ascent in prayer as being so ordered and interdependent, we must not fall into rationalistic error: There is no limit to the Creator's powers, and He can give as He chooses, within or without this ordered chain of progress. (In the terms he is here employing, Guigo shows how constantly the language of the liturgy is in his mind: when he writes *Deus, cujus potentiae non est terminus* (God whose mercies are unlimited), he is recalling the collect that appears in the Carthusian Missal in the Mass *'pro gratiarum actione,'* and today in the feast of Our Lady, Mother of Mercy, in the Roman Rite—*Deus cujus misericordiae non est numerus* (God whose mercies are unnumbered)—it is noteworthy that most of our scribes have sought to substitute *numerus* for *terminus*—and, a few lines later, when he says, using the hyperbole from St. Matthew, that God raises sons for Abraham from the very stones, he may have in mind the votice nuptial Mass of the Gelasian and Leonian Sacramentaries, where in the solemn blessing we read: . . . *qui Adae comitem tuis manibus addidisti, cuius ex ossibus ossa crescentia parem formam admirabili diversitate signarent* . . . (. . . who with your hands added his companion to Adam, from whose bones were to grow bones which might give to the one form a wonderful diversity . . .). God, as the proverb says, 'gives the ox by the horn' (in fact, the commoner form of the proverb says that God does not send the ox by the horn, against which the author of *The Cloud of Unknowing* was to protest, making again Guigo's point, that it is not for our finite powers of judgment to put limits to the Lord's generosity).[46] Yet we must not presume upon this divine generosity, making it an excuse for our own parsimony. It is for us, if we wish for the fullness of God's gifts, to give to this work of contemplation all that we possess. But still we must be on our guard, lest this very plenitude with which we may be endowed become the occasion of reversal, of 'a violent plunge from the very heavens into the depths'. This echoes what William of St. Thierry had written in Chapter 5 of *De natura et dignitate amoris,* where William makes explicit what Guigo allows us to infer, that a presumptuous reliance on our own powers is the surest way of inviting such a fall.[47] We cannot always remain upon the heights, but we must retrace our way by the same degrees on which we climbed, in gentle and orderly manner.

In Chapter 15, 'Four Obstacles to These Degrees', Guigo continues his reflections on the circumstances under which a contemplative will turn aside from his pursuit of mystical union. He is here closely following what Hugh of St. Victor says in *De arca Noe morali* II, that sometimes such a one will be forced to desert the secret places of the heart through human infirmity, sometimes through necessity. Hugh goes on to say that those who leave the ark of contemplation for the sake of worldly pleasures are unclean beasts (this is Guigo's fourth, blameworthy obstacle), those who do so out of necessity are beasts, but clean (here we have Guigo's second, tolerable obstacle). And when Hugh pursues his theme to observe that 'those who take upon them the care of government in the Church, and emerge from the silence of an inward peace to public life, not out of ambition but in obedience, are like Noah',[48] he shows us very clearly what is in Guigo's mind when he writes of excusable, unavoidable necessity. He too was thinking of the dilemma and the conflict when one vowed to the contemplative life is called on to accept high office: We have already mentioned his reluctance to allow Hugh of Avalon to accept the summons of Henry II of England to the priorate of Witham, and Hugh's biographer tells us that later he refused to be named as bishop of Lincoln, until the Grande Chartreuse had put him under the obedience of the archbishop of Canterbury.[49]

Guigo imagines the reproaches that God will heap upon such a faithless soul: 'What more should I have done for you that I have not done?' The ultimate source of this passage, obviously, is the use in the Good Friday *Reproaches* of the Old Testament narratives of God's fidelity to Israel; and Guigo may also have had in mind Anselm's *Meditatio Redemptionis Humanae.*[50] Yet, even if we are so mad as to make this ruinous bargain, still let us refrain from despair, but hasten in repentance to our merciful healer.

The manuscripts make no division between the end of this chapter and the brief epilogue, addressed again to Gervase, in which Guigo asks for his prayers if ever the veil of the sanctuary is drawn, so that Gervase sees God, that the Lord who listens may bid Guigo also to the vision of Him.

The Ladder of Monks

THE MIDDLE ENGLISH VERSION:
A LADDER OF FOUR RUNGS

In three fifteenth-century manuscripts, Cambridge University Library Ff. vi. 33, Bodleian Library Douce 322 and British Museum Harleian 1706, a Middle English version of the *Ladder,* 'A Ladder of Four Rungs by Which Men May Well Climb to Heaven', is found. This version has been edited by Professor Hodgson as Appendix B of her edition of *Deonise Hid Divinite.*[51]

It depends, for its Latin text, upon some manuscript corresponding to Wilmart's Group IV, a group that completely rearranges the original text. Some sixty manuscripts, well over half of those listed or referred to by Wilmart, belong to this class, including twelve in English libraries. Such manuscripts all lack the prologue and epilogue. They begin with Chapter II, followed by Chapter III, as far as 'delight in the sweetness which we have found' (11.17–53). They follow this with Chapters XII–XIV, 'Reading comes first, and is as it were the foundation . . . until at last he can see the God of gods in Sion' (ll. 319–421). The omitted section follows immediately: from Chapter IV, 'I hear the words read: "Blessed are the pure in heart . . . " ' to Chapter X, ' . . . and before our taste is satisfied He withdraws' (ll. 56–279). The Middle English version derives from a manuscript in the (a) class of Group IV,[52] so that the final portion of the text corresponds to 'See now, you have had a little taste . . . if you wish often to enjoy your spouse's company' (ll. 280–309), and 'But let such a man beware . . . he will lighten the load which weighs us down' (ll. 426–97).

The intention of this rearrangement appears to have been to make the treatise less schematic and less obviously didactic, and thus more suitable for devotional reading, though it antedated the dissemination of Pierre D'Ailly's recension of the treatise among the Brothers of the Common Life. Where Guigo treats in logical order of the four rungs successively, citing the text 'Blessed are the pure in heart' quite early in his exposition as a simple example of the function of each rung, the original editor of the Group IV text pays no heed to Guigo's scheme; instead he makes the reflections on this text the hinge of the whole treatise: Reading and meditation bring the soul to the realization that purification, active and passive, is the essential prerequisite for the grace of contemplation, while prayer will obtain this grace.

The English translator carries this process even further, as can be seen from his translation, or rather adaptation, of the passage at the beginning of Chapter IV, 'I hear the words read "Blessed are the pure in heart . . . " '. In St. Matthew's gospel, Christ says: 'Blessed are the pure of heart, for they will see God'. There are only a few words here, but they are of great power and sweetness; they are most efficacious, and open the way to life. When a man hears these words sound in his ears, and sees them with his spiritual eyes, he speaks to his soul and says: 'It seems that these words can open a way to

God. I will attempt this in my own heart, and find with His guidance how I can understand and obtain this purity, for it is a great treasure, and truly makes those who have it gain the joy of heaven. And Christ Himself promises them that they will see God, and this sight alone is the fulfillment of all joy for all who are the friends of God.'

His occasional minor omissions, which amount to no more than half a dozen sentences, are all made in order to present the treatise in a less formal fashion. From the very beginning, he never scruples to round out the terse style and brief content of his original. His first addition to his text occurs after the second sentence, when he explains that 'This was the ladder which Jacob saw', and goes on to declare what is signified by the angelic traffic up and down the ladder—the ministration of angels in the work of contemplation, and why God is leaning over it. Again, he is at pains, at the end of Chapter X, to enlarge on Guigo's passing reference to Jacob and the touch of the angel, and to offer at length the traditional contemplative exegesis of the episode in Genesis.

He is even more anxious than was Guigo to make it clear that love always leads in matters contemplative. In place of his author's simile 'by flying above us with wings outspread . . . ' towards the end of Chapter X, he introduces the following comparison: 'Almighty God acts toward his lovers in time of contemplation as does an innkeeper who has good wine to sell toward discerning drinkers who will drink his wine freely and spend generously. He can recognize their quality when he sees them in the street. He goes up to them quietly, whispers to them and tells them that he has a claret which will be to their taste. He takes them to his house and lets them sample it. When they have tried it, and think that the wine is good and very pleasing to them, they then drink every day and every night, and the more they drink, the more they are able to drink. They have acquired such a taste for that drink that they do not think of any other wine; all they want is to drink their fill and have as much as they want of this wine. And so they spend all their money, and then they sell or pawn their clothes and everything they can so as to go on drinking for as long as they like. And sometimes it is like that with God's lovers. When once they had tasted this honeyed wine, which is God's sweetness, they found such delight in it that they behaved like drunken men, spending everything they had, giving themselves up to fasting, vigils and other penances. And when they had no more to spend, they pawned their possessions, as the Apostles, martyrs and young virgins did in their time. Some gave their bodies to be burned, some let their heads be cut off, some suffered their breasts to be cut from their bodies, some were flayed alive, some were torn in pieces by wild horses; and all that they did they thought little of compared with their longing for that everlasting joy which they desired to possess fully in eternal life. But this delight is only given us here to taste, and all who desire to possess it fully must follow Christ step by step, again and again moving him with their love, just as these drinkers do with the innkeeper. Therefore, when God sends any spiritual delight to your soul, think that he is speaking to you, whispering in your ear and saying: "Take this little now, and taste how sweet I am. But if you want to experience fully what you have often tasted, run after me, following the sweet scent of my ointment. Lift up your heart to me, where I am sitting on my Father's right hand, and there you will see me, not as in a mirror but face to face. And then you will have in full all that you want, for ever, of the joy which you have tasted. And no one will rob you of that joy or delight".'

Equally characteristic of the English translator's style and approach is his addition to Guigo's brief reference in Chapter V to the true wisdom, which is the gift of contemplation. Guigo had said that the sweetness of contemplation was withheld from pagan philosophers, notwithstanding that they were able to arrive at a knowledge of the highest and truest good by the use of their reason. The anti-intellectualism of the translator, traditionally drawn from the spiritual exegesis

of Matthew 11:25, is even more emphatic: 'For this understanding we must open not our ears but our hearts. This
understanding is hidden from the wise men of the world, and
it is shown and revealed to the humble and the meek so that
they can truly understand and experience it. Thus, great
power comes out of the humility which is so precious to
recognize and to gain, which cannot be learned by human
understanding, or heard with the body's ears or described in
words. This spiritual understanding God has kept only for His
chosen ones, so that all rational creatures know and understand that there is a master teaching and instructing in
heaven, who teaches true wisdom and learning to His chosen
scholars and enlightens them within through His grace, and
makes them know and experience that to which no worldly
understanding can attain. You can see this if you will look at ✗
a simple poor old woman who has little intelligence and who
cannot say either the Our Father or the Creed properly, yet
in a few moments she will experience such delight that all her
heart melts in blissful sorrow, so that she cannot pray without
tears and sorrowful longing. Who, do you think, teaches her
to pray like this? It is not worldly understanding, but grace
from above. Similarly some poor simple laborer who is so
stupid that he could not argue anything out to save his life,
can still attain to this teaching and this wisdom as perfectly
as the wisest man in the land, whoever he may be, provided
that he does what is in him. Truly he may well be called the
best of teachers who is known for teaching wisdom, not
through human understanding, to the unwise, making them
feel and understand that which no man can attain through the
knowledge of this world, provided only that man does his
part and inclines his heart's ear to listen to that teaching.
This wisdom is nothing but the gift of God; and He has
reserved it to Himself, to give to those He wishes.'

It has already been noticed that there are numerous striking parallels between *A Ladder of Four Rungs* and the tone
and temper of the *Cloud of Unknowing* and the treatises

attributed to the *Cloud's* author. The language and style of
these interpolations seem to indicate the late fourteenth century as the date of the translation, which loses nothing from
the point of view of skill and ease in its handling of the original, in comparison with, say, the author of the *Cloud's*
translation of the *Benjamin Minor* of Richard of St. Victor,
or Walter Hilton's version of the *Stimulus amoris.*

By far the longest interpolation introduced by the English
translator is an excursus on grace. Its relative simplicity and
the clarity of its language, together with the use of popular
exempla (that of the dog and the water is, in the West, as old
as Aesop) suggests as its author a cleric accustomed to
addressing unlearned audiences, and one with a high degree
of catechetical expertise, who knows how to explain difficult
points of doctrine without confusing his hearers with the
terminology and tortuous arguments of the Schools. His purpose is simply to explain the role of divine grace in the spiritual life. After translating Guigo's Latin from Chapter XIII,
'But if there be any good in us, He performs it in us, but
not without us; for St. Paul says: "We are God's helpers" for
our own good. That is to say, we open our hearts when He
sends us the riches of His grace, and we do everything that is
in us to hold it and guard it.' The translator continues: 'But
because we can do nothing which will please Him or save our
souls without His grace, therefore we must say something in
this little book about the grace of God. You must understand
that there are three graces which come from God. The first is
a common grace, given by God to all His creatures. This is the
help which God in His goodness gives to all His creatures,
to each one separately according to its nature, so that they
can move and feel, and without His grace they can do nothing: without it even their natural life would fail. You see,
for example, that water is hot through the strength of fire,
and if the fire is drawn from it, it loses its heat and naturally
grows cold. It is just like this with every creature, as
St. Augustine testifies. "For just as all creatures come from

nothing and are made of nothing, unless they are sustained and preserved by His grace they will immediately return to nothing." St. Paul understood this well when he said: "By the grace of God I am what I am." It was as if he had said: "That I exist, that I have life, that I can see, feel, walk or stand: all is of God's grace."

"There is a second and more special grace of God. This grace God offers only to man, to take if he wishes; and this grace always stands at the gates of our heart, and knocks on our free will for admission, as it says in the Book of Revelations: "Behold I stand at the door and knock. Whoever hears my voice and opens the gates to me, I shall enter into him, and I shall sup with him and he with me." You see here the liberality of our Lord, who in His merciful grace offers Himself so meekly. And this grace is called God's free gift to man. Man should accept this second grace when God sends it, and prepare himself through its help, that he may be worthy to receive the gift of the Holy Spirit, which moves a man to good and calls him away from evil.

"You must understand that two things are necessary for the salvation of man's soul. The first is the grace of which we have just spoken, and the second is free will. Without these two, no human creature can achieve his soul's salvation, no matter what else he can do. For free will is of no use without grace, nor is grace unless there is free will helping and assenting. St. Augustine affirms this, when he says: "He who created you without your help, will not justify you without your help'. And though man's free will cannot create grace in man, nonetheless man can do what is in his power: cast out the old leaven, which is the old corrupting sin that separates man from grace, and so prepare himself to receive this grace. As you know, you cannot of your own power light up a room, but you can open the window and let in the sunshine; and if you shut your eyes to the sunlight, who is to blame if you do not see? And if you will not open your mouth to take food, you are wrong to complain if you are hungry. God says

to you: "Be sure that if you open your mouth I will fill it".
This means: "Open your heart to Me, and I will fill it with
My grace". And therefore a man who has not this grace is
much to blame, for, as St. Augustine says: "Man does not
lack grace because God does not give it to him". The meaning
of this is that man does not do everything in his power to
receive it, because if he did, it would come to him and dwell
with him. Therefore, St. Augustine says: "God in His immense liberality fills all His creatures according to their
capacity". Therefore, if man will open the gates of his heart
to this grace which moves and calls him, and, by his free
will, allow it to enter freely, it will dwell wholly with him
and make him shew by his deeds that grace is his true companion. And therefore the Apostle says: "The grace of God
was not idle in me". No more was it, because he shewed by
his external works what God's grace achieved in him. This is
exactly what grace does in those in whom it makes its dwelling, because it cannot be idle, for it must necessarily perform
the works which the Father of heaven sent it to do. St. Augustine speaks about this grace, and says: "This grace is always ready for me, if it finds me ready; wherever I go, it never
leaves me unless I leave it first."

'God is like a partner performing half His works. He acts
with us like a partner who wants to make a profit. He gives
His grace and we give our works, like merchants seeking their
due profit. And He puts forward many great claims to the
love and the reverence He should have as His share from
man, but we like miserable cheats deprive Him fraudulently.
We think that the gain is all ours, but we lose everything, for
we commit injury and fraud, we give our love to the devil and
our reverence to the world and to the flesh, and so our love is
withheld from our gracious partner. As St. John says in his
Epistle: "Do not love the world, nor those things which are
in the world. Whoever loves the world, the love of the Father
is not in him; for everything that is in the world is desire of
the eye and the pride of life, which is not of the Father but

of the world. And the world will pass, and the desire of it."
These things are loved against the counsels of our Lord God,
our partner, and we defraud Him of His share which He
bought at so great a price, that is with the blood of the
undefiled Lamb, Christ Jesus. We separate ourselves willfully
from the joy of the Lord, as the dog did which carried a
cheese by the water's edge, and as he looked into the water,
he saw the reflection of the cheese and opened his mouth to
take it, and the cheese fell out. And so he lost what he had
and what he wanted to have. Therefore God says to such
people through the prophet Isaias: "I shall not give My glory
to another," that is, "I shall not share the love and honor
paid to Me with any others but those who are My true
servants." So be like a true partner to God, and let Him have
His share.

'The third grace is more special, for it is not given to all
men, but only to them who open the gates of their hearts and
prepare their free will to receive it. This grace is the gift of
the Holy Spirit which moves man to perform good works.
God gives this grace to man with which to win merit. Without this grace nothing that we do is meritorious. This grace
has three elements: the first, itself a grace freely given,
moving the free will; the second, the will assenting; and the
third, God creating and giving this grace. It is the sign of
God's special love toward them to whom He sends it. This
grace makes a man patient whenever he might be angry, and
makes him endure meekly loss of his possessions and his
worldly friends, bodily injuries, sickness, and penance for
past sins without inward murmuring. It makes a man per-
severe in goodness; it makes him beware of evil and able to
recognize everything that is good. God gives it to man here
as an earnest, if only he will keep it, for everlasting joy. The
angel in the Book of Revelations says of this grace: "Hold
what you have"; as if he said: "If you wish to have that joy
which is everlasting, hold fast to that grace which God has
sent to you, for it opens the way to joy".'

The distinction between the grace that is 'common', bestowed by God on all His creatures, and that which is 'more special', follows St. Thomas: 'One form of God's love for His creatures is common, for "He loves all things that are," as is said in Wisdom 11:25 . . . but He has another love which is special, and it is through this that He draws the rational creature, above the condition of its nature, to share in His divine goodness.'[53] It is frequently asserted by St. Augustine that it is God's love, His goodness, His grace that sustains all creation. 'If He withdrew His goodness from created things, they would immediately cease to exist';[54] 'If this same goodness were withdrawn from His creative action, which gives origin, form and life to all living creatures, not only would they cease to reproduce themselves, but even what was produced would return to nothingness.'[55] It is of this second that the English quotation seems to be a paraphrase.

The further special grace, offered only to man, is called 'God's free gift': That is, it is created grace, offered by God to man, to take or reject as he wishes; it is sanctifying grace, the first condition for merit, as Bradwardine had insisted against Ockham and 'the modern Pelagians'; it is St. Thomas's 'gift of justifying grace, above all else directing man to that good which is the object of the will, so that man is moved toward it by a movement of the will, which is a movement of his free choice'.[56] With the help of this special grace man prepares himself for a grace yet more special, the gift of the Holy Spirit.

Then we have a résumé of another closely related topic, the necessity for salvation of the interaction of divine grace and man's free will. In the mid-fourteenth century this had been argued again, with great vehemence and a certain lack of balance, by Bradwardine, who had reaffirmed St. Augustine's teaching, and relied heavily on the places where Augustine insisted, against Pelagius, that without grace man was free only to do evil. Here, however, we are only given the classical, 'Thus He who made you without your help will not justify you without your help.'[57] The interpolator follows this with a reminder of the falseness of the belief, originally Pelagian but frequently reappearing, that the human will itself can create grace in man; and in his metaphor of our inability to give light, but our power to open a window to admit the light, he is probably recalling the *Ennaratio in Ps. 118, 72,* where Augustine says that it is neither the carpenter who makes the window nor the sun shining in which illumines the house, but God who created the sun and the man.[58] Then he reminds us of one aspect of Augustine's doctrine on the question why grace is not equally given: As it stands, the statement 'Man does not lack grace because God does not give it to him' could misrepresent Augustine, but not if we read it in conjunction with the passages (e.g. *De Correptione et Gratia 11*)[59] where he teaches that if man lacks grace, it is punishment for sin.

Finally, the interpolation describes the third, more special grace, the gift of the Holy Spirit with which man wins merit, without which nothing that we do is meritorious. Here again, it follows St. Thomas, 'Can a man merit eternal life without grace?'[60] and Thomas's marshaling of the older authorities, notably St. Paul and St. Augustine, and it ends with an oblique allusion to one of Augustine's greatest contributions to the debate upon grace, his teachings concerning the gift of final perseverance.

THE MEDITATIONS

It is evident that the *Meditations* gained nothing like the popularity or the circulation of the *Ladder.* Only seven manuscripts have been found containing all of them; Wilmart added an eighth to his list, Paris, Bibliothèque Sainte-Geneviève 1367, containing only Meditations VII and VIII.[61] The oldest, Vatican Lat. 134 (V), of the early thirteenth century, states that the author is 'the venerable Guido, prior of the Chartreuse', and British Museum Royal 8. F. i (R), a thirteenth-century manuscript of English provenance, calls him 'Hugo, prior to the Chartreuse'. Four (three of them thirteenth century, and one if not two of English provenance) attribute the work to Bernard, and Bibliothèque Nationale Latin 3761 (P 2), also of the thirteenth century, has no ascription. When Wilmart published his findings on the two Guigos and their works, these *Meditations* had not been edited. Using MSS H (British Museum Harley 47), R and V, he gave several extracts, and his opinion that their author could not possibly be Guigo I, himself the author of a different group of meditations. This second group appeared to him entirely different from the first, and he discerned in them 'a gentle, calm and pervasive piety'. Although to him the influence of Augustine was manifest, none the less he was satisfied that they must be by a contemporary of Bernard, and saw no reason to question their ascription of Guigo II.[62] Encouraged by Wilmart's notices of the *Meditations,* M.-M. Davy in 1932–34 published what claims to be a critical text, using, in addition to those listed by him, MSS P1 and P2.[63] But this edition is full of mistakes and wholly unreliable.

It may be significant that so few manuscripts survive which contain texts of all the works attributed to Guigo. It would seem that neither he nor any contemporary in the Grande Chartreuse thought it important to collect and edit in a single volume everything he had written. The ideas, and the style in which they are conveyed, mark the *Meditations* as an earlier work than the *Ladder,* but in the *Ladder* we find no cross references to his earlier treatment of the same topics in the *Meditations,* perhaps for the good reason that Guigo himself regarded their fuller and deeper second treatment as superseding the first. None the less, we can perceive considerable unity of thought in both and little diversity of method.

Both works show Guigo wholly wedded to the extraction from Scripture of its spiritual sense. At the end of Chapter 8 of the *Ladder* he writes that unitive prayer can only be learned ' . . . from the book of experience where God's grace itself is the teacher. Otherwise it is of no use for the reader to search in earthly books: there is little sweetness in the study of the literal sense, unless there be a commentary, which is found in the heart, to reveal the inward sense'. The opposing technique, the insistence upon the literal and historical senses which had experienced a powerful revival in his own age, had no attractions for him; and already in the *Meditations* we see a scholar, with a ready command of the Bible, to whom it comes naturally to present his ideas clothed in Scripture phrases which, for him, have as their most inward meaning what they can tell us of how the soul draws ever closer to God. For modern readers this constant quotation and allusion may make the text dense and at times obscure, slow and hard to read, but that is exactly the effect Guigo aims at. What he writes in Meditation X, 'For how can anything be understood which is thought about only rarely and carelessly?' is good advice for all who study him. Even so, in the *Ladder* we seem to have the writing of a more mature hand: He is better able to select, and he relies more on his own independent powers of expression, less upon authority. But the dominant ideas are the same. As will be shown when his use of other authors in the *Meditations* is discussed, he is all the time directed by his search for the recognition and cultivation of the stages of the interior life in which the soul may become one with God; and it is very clear that he had already begun to explore one idea, suggested to him by the imagery of both Testaments, the analogies between the soul's assimilation of divine truths and the processes of mastication and digestion, which are only partially presented in Meditations X, XI and XII, but are fully worked out in Chapters 3 to 6 of the *Ladder.*

But even if Guigo did consider that the *Ladder* in its treatment of this topic replaced what was in the *Meditations,* we can still profitably read the two together; and in Meditation XI we find one most fruitful notion that does not reappear in the *Ladder.* The previous meditation, concerned with Christ's body, and with how, by following Him, imitating Him, clinging to Him, we may possess the whole of Him and become one body with Him, has used the analogy of chewing and digestion: To become one with Christ is a slow and laborious process of cultivation of the spiritual faculties. But in XI the processes of drinking are contrasted. This is easy and quick; and so too are we one with Christ without any great labor, when we drink of His chalice, when we are united to Him by sharing His sufferings, and in this union find rest for our souls. 'To hunger and thirst' has its place also in the *Ladder,* but this potent thought is found in the *Meditations* alone.

DOCTRINE AND SOURCES

Meditation I is written in praise of the solitary life; and it examines the interior, psychological hindrances to solitude.

Guigo shows his familiarity with the classical Western treat-
ments, from Cassian onward, of this topic, and in particular,
he is indebted to Gregory, who in Book V of the *Moralia*
quotes Job 4:12, 'Your words are so softly spoken . . . ' and
interprets the text as Guigo does: 'When then God breathes
silently upon man's thought and lifts it up, His hidden word
of the Spirit speaks silently to the ear of the heart'.[64] And
when Guigo addresses Christ as the exemplar of the hidden,
solitary life that can be lived in the crowd, he is probably
recalling another place, Book XXVIII, where Gregory had
written: 'Though the active and contemplative lives are far
apart, when the Redeemer took flesh and came among us He
lived and joined together both lives. He worked miracles in
the city, but He passed whole nights in prayer upon the
mountain . . .'.[65] But in this first meditation, and thereafter,
Guigo is even more in the debt of a modern writer, his pre-
cursor Guigo I of the Grande Chartreuse. He, in Chapter 80
of his *Consuetudines,* writes that 'Jesus who is both God
and Lord . . . before He had preached or given any sign was
as it were tested by His temptations and His fastings in solitude, when the Scriptures tell us that He left the crowds
which followed after Him and climbed the mountain to pray.
Then when the time of His Passion was approaching, He left
the apostles so that He could make His prayer alone, showing
us by this powerful example how much prayer is helped by
solitude, because then He did not wish the company even of
the apostles whilst He prayed.'[66] And in this same chapter
Guigo I also uses the text from Lamentations which introduces this Meditation I, 'It is good for a man to have borne
your burden since he was young; let him sit alone and be
silent', and he says that Jeremiah, finding that his earthly
companions are a hindrance to those graces, especially of the
gift of tears, which he seeks, is a type of the contemplative,
'signifying almost everything which is best in our way of life,
quiet and solitude, silence and the seeking of gifts from on
high'.[67] Guigo I had quoted, 'Let him sit alone and be

silent' earlier, in Chapter 14, where, dealing with the Carthusian obligations to the souls of the departed, he explains that Masses for benefactors are rarely sung among them 'because our first care and aim is to preserve the silence and solitude of our cell . . . and it is our opinion that there is nothing in the exercise of our religious discipline more difficult to preserve than the solitary's silence and peace. This is why St. Augustine says: "There is no work harder for those who love this world than not to work".'[68] What is implicit here is fully explained in Meditation I: To attain to true solitude, the contemplative must go beyond separation from the world and from sin. He must pursue an inward solitude, which we will learn by imitating his Saviour, carrying his burden, humbling himself, and so finding silence and peace and a lifting up of the spirit of God. As he concluded this meditation, Guigo II probably had in mind the prayer to be said over novices at their profession, which we find in Chapter 25 of the *Consuetudines,* where Christ, who did not scorn to call sinners to Him, saying, 'Come to me, all you who are burdened down, and I will refresh you', is asked to make His call to this new member of His flock so clear that he may be worthy to be counted among the Lord's sheep, that he may follow no one else, hear no other call, but follow after the one true shepherd.

In the second meditation, Guigo describes the first effects upon a beginner of this chosen life of poverty and solitude, and he does this in the classical manner of which he was already master, illustrating his own spiritual state by the juxtaposition of texts from the Psalms, Jeremiah and Job, all of which were familiar to him and his readers in liturgical contexts which give them heightened significance. All others dear to him have forsaken the young religious, and he must rely upon God alone. Guigo does not develop this theme on the usual lines, which would be familiar to him from such works as Guigo I's *Letter on the Solitary Life,*[69] where the benefits and compensations which will attend this sense of dereliction and deprivation are stressed. He is content merely to describe his present state, without looking for consolations. He then compares himself with one of the types in the Old Law of such affliction, Anna bewailing her sterility and refusing the comfort which her husband proffered. Her tears were acceptable to God, who blessed her with a child. So this meditation ends by implying that God reward with spiritual fruitfulness the solitary who patiently endures this season of barrenness and does not seek for any help, except that which God will give to those who faithfully pursue their vocation.

We must read Meditations II and III together, if we are to extract from III its fullness of meaning. The solitary, in his spiritual poverty, contemplates the inexhaustible riches of the Lord and asks to be fed from His table with the true food of the soul, the praises of God on which alone Jerusalem, the city of peace, is fed. Here Guigo is anticipating his final meditation, in which he will develop more fully this theme of the word of God as the 'bread of angels', and he shows already his command of the style and method that make the two Eucharistic meditations, X and XI, so remarkable. His choice of illustrative figures is always apt, and they are skillfully combined to provide meanings as profound as terse—this is particularly true of the passage describing the feeding of Elias by the widow of Sarepta and the raven. Many of Guigo's 'allegories' are traditional—the raven as a type of the contumacious sinner is found in Rabanus Maurus's *Allegoriae*,[70] for example—but Guigo enriches them by his striking elaborations: the raven, the sinner, who yet fed Elias, is equated with Zacheus, the tax gatherer, perched in the tree, commanded to descend and to feed Christ. This passage ends with an observation that may at first seem obscure: 'And he did this in the evening, at twilight, when it may be truly said, "morning and evening make one day".' But one theme constantly present in this meditation was already introduced by II, that of progress in the contemplative life. The soul has now emerged from its merely negative poverty and glimpses the riches with which God can reward it, but it is still in the twilight, it has not yet emerged into the full light of God's day. For this, the sinner, the raven, has to be purified before it can become the dove, the fit bride of the spouse. (Here Guigo is very close in his interpretation of Canticles to the Cistercian Gilbert of Hoyland in his Sermon XXIII.)[71] This purification is death, by the 'new sprinkling', baptism, and it is renewal, by the 'new food', made from the first fruits—that is, of penance and mortification—through which humility and simplicity are acquired.

This humility and simplicity, this opening of the heart to the Lord's gifts, are strongly contrasted in Meditation IV with the heart's present hardness, its disquiet and its instability as it first seeks for God. Again, many of Guigo's images and ideas are traditional. That our hearts of stone will be replaced by hearts of flesh, as Ezechiel prays, will be accomplished when the heart melts and expands in the burning heat of divine love, we find, for instance, in Peter of Celle.[72] And Guerric of Igny, in his Sermon III, *Of Spiritual Rest,* says, as Guigo does in the beginning of this Meditation IV, that if God, the lover and the giver of peace, is to find a resting place in us, our hearts must be endowed with 'rest' and 'steadiness', for it is the cause of great harm that we should resemble the sinful Jerusalem which the Book of Proverbs compares with the wanton, straying, gossiping women of the streets.[73] This 'rest' will be found, Guerric teaches, by the affliction of the body.[74] And when Guigo tells us that the Spirit, coming to prepare His abode in us, will found it on the fear of the Lord, he may be recalling Bruno's letter to Raoul de Verde, the future archbishop of Rheims, concerning Raoul's vow to become a solitary, where Bruno says that if the love of God does not dispose us to necessary acts of renunciation, we should at least be moved by necessity and by fear.[75] Guerric of Igny, too, uses, as Guigo does, the citations from Galatians, 'All who belong to Christ have crucified

their flesh,' and Psalm 118, 'Chasten my flesh with fear of
you', and says that it is the fear of God that will chasten and
crucify our evil inclinations.[76]

Manifestly, Guigo is not merely concerned with 'cruci-
fixion' as a means of overcoming vice and concupiscence.
That will be achieved by what he calls 'the first cross', the
mortification of the flesh; but this fear of God, which will
reorder our spiritual lives, will be obtained by a second cross,
'the cross of the soul'; and there is yet a third, 'a cross of the
spirit which is love', and it is this third cross that will restore
to us hearts of flesh. Guigo's allusion to the legend of St. Andrew helps us to see in what direction his thoughts are tend-
ing. It was love for his Master and longing to imitate him in
all things, 'as far as death, death even on a cross', which
made the crucified Andrew pray 'Lord Jesus Christ, do not
scatter them to free your servant from that cross on which he
hangs for your name's sake'.[77] Christ suffered because of His
great love, and as we suffer, for love of Him, in the spirit, we
shall come closer to Him, piercing in prayer the cloud
between Him and us.[78]

The thought and the imagery here belong to a refined and
wholly orthodox form of Dionysianism, of which William of
St. Thierry was the chief exponent in the twelfth century;
and Guigo shows, in a few terse sentences, how well he has
mastered William's thought. The cloud between it and God,
which the soul must penetrate, suggests the cloud that for
six days hid Moses on Mount Sinai, till on the seventh day
the Lord called to him from out of the cloud. The six days,
Guigo says, signify the six virtues by which Moses ascended
to the seventh and highest, wisdom. And so by the first and
second crosses we achieve and exercise fear, reverence and
knowledge, fortitude, counsel and understanding. But the
third, the cross of love by which we attain to the very
presence of God, 'transcends all this'. and in God's presence
the soul, 'gathered into the unity of love, may sleep in true
peace and take its rest'. Here we have, in brief but in a form

unambiguous and unexaggerated, the teaching of the thirteenth-century Dionysian spirituals—the Victorine Thomas Gallus, and the two Carthusians Hugh de Balma and Guigo de Pont. What is significant is that Guigo avoids the extreme form of anti-intellectualism that critics of later Western mysticism were to resist so strongly, e.g. in the doctrine of Eckhart and Ruysbroek, fearing that it would encourage false passivity.

It is beyond doubt that Meditation IV, though it is occupied with the whole progress, from its early stages, of contemplative life, was written by one who was himself already far advanced in the practice of unitive prayer.

In Meditation V, Guigo seeks and finds analogies for God's work, as he re-creates through grace the human soul, in his first work of creation as it is described in Genesis. There are precedents for such analogies. Guigo may have known the *Treatise of the Works of the Six Days* of Arnold of Boneval (†1156), in which he compares the newly created land, 'empty and void', with the first state of man, 'for although he was formed in innocency, he was not yet reformed, the body of our wretchedness had not yet become like to the body assumed in his love by God . . . The earth was empty of that fullness of blessedness which it was to receive, for it had no one to possess it; it was void, having no beauty, for that on which God does not shine His light is formless . . . and so the first light came, thrusting back darkness and establishing day, driving out ignorance and with wisdom purifying the mind.'[79] Here is the same idea as Guigo develops, but it is noteworthy that he, to express it fully, has recourse to the Old Latin version, the 'other translation' to which he refers, of Genesis 1:2, where instead of 'empty and void' we read 'invisible and orderless'.[80] It is this idea of the formlessness of chaos that suggests to Guigo man's ignorance of the true image in which he must be re-created: and this re-creation is an endless process, very like what Eckhart and Tauler were to teach of 'the birth in the soul of the Word'. This is the ceaseless work the Son ascribed to the Father; and God is the great abyss, 'beyond all that sense can perceive' to which the abyss, the soul, sunk deep and unillumined, calls aloud. Guigo certainly here recalled what Bruno in his commentary on Psalm 41 had said of the abyss as 'the depths of a future and eternal damnation',[81] and there may be other discernible influences—Hugh of St. Victor, in *De arca Noe morali*, on the soul's 'blindness',[82] and Augustine, in the *Ennarationes in Johannem*, on Lazarus as a type of the soul's rebirth in grace.[83] But the main conception and the execution are Guigo's own, a strikingly original contribution to the Western literature of 'image theology'.

The next meditation continues and amplifies the ideas of V, and again, the influence of Arnold of Boneval is plain. In his *Tractatus* he tells us that the Spirit of God moved over the waters so that there should be nothing wanting, nothing of weakness in our creation. The Spirit forms and fosters our rational appetites, helps our weakness, makes fruitful our sterility, excites our devotion; and then the soul is enabled in the light of truth to distinguish between what is carnal and what is spiritual, 'as if between the waters on high and the waters below'.[84] The phrase, 'the waters on high and the waters below', may have been suggested to Arnold by the account of creation in Genesis, Chapter 1, but its application to the work of creation and the analogy with man's re-generation seem to be original, and they provide the beginning of Guigo's Meditation VI. But here again, Guigo has changed and deepened Arnold's thought. Although in the *Tractatus* we shall also find Guigo's image of the waters of human nature becoming through sin a lake of mire and filth, what we do not find there is the concept of *regiratio* (turning back again), of the return in the cycle to God, the one source, to which Guigo so aptly applies the analogy suggested by Arnold. As in the previous meditation, we see how much Guigo has made his own modes of thought with which most Western theologians were unfamiliar for at least another century.

Dom Jean Leclercq, characterizing the monasticism of Cluny and of the other reforming houses, including the Grande Chartreuse in its early years, has said that they held before them, ' . . . as the most perfect model of the virtues which the Church should preserve in the world, the Virgin Mary. In her were united to the highest degree gentleness and chastity, in her was found a perfect renunciation of the two vices which are the source of all other ills, egoism and lechery . . . and she was not only exemplar but protectress, whose aid they were all accustomed to invoke: she is that "advocate" from whom one can ask help, that sovereign lady to whom one does well to render homage.'[85] These traits are exceptionally well illustrated by Guigo's Meditations VII, VIII and IX. In each some special aspects of Mary's role in the work of redemption are considered, and are expounded according to the twofold method he could employ so well. Contemporary devotions provide him with his terms, and these are explained by reference back to the characters and events of the Old Testament which traditional exegesis claimed as Marian types.

Meditation VII hails our Lady as consolation of the afflicted, mother of mercy; and Guigo sees her type in Rebecca. He has, in fact, here transferred to Mary what Ambrose, in *De Abraham* I, said was typical in Chapter 24 of Genesis of the Church, the 'virgin very beautiful', 'unknown to man' except to her spouse, Christ, bearing in her vessel the waters of grace to purify the lives of men, not only the just, but also the sinners who are the camels which Rebecca watered.[86] Aelred of Rievaulx, a near-contemporary, some of whose writings Guigo certainly knew, in his *Sermo VIII in Annunitiatione* says that Rebecca, like Rachel, is the type of Mary, Abraham's servant the type of Gabriel, though he does not develop this; but elsewhere in this same sermon he does say that, sweet as it might be to us to speculate on how great our Lady's physical beauty, suggested to us in

Genesis 24, may be, we ought to interpret this 'virgin very beautiful' in a spiritual sense.[87] Guigo does so: Mary is 'beautiful indeed' because the Holy Spirit filled her heart with light, so that she repels the devil, 'that vilest of creatures, seducer of minds, who . . . has always fled away from you'; and he sees in Rebecca, offering the travelers a resting place in her father's spacious mansion, a type of Mary as she forms the way on which the banished children of Eve will return to their true home. As he compares the soul with a benighted traveler, exposed to the terrors and perils of the wilderness unless our Lady lead him into the Father's house, Guigo may have had in mind another concept of image theology, the idea, neo-Platonic in origin, of human existence as the 'region of unlikeness' in which man wanders exiled because he has lost his likeness to his Creator which was the Lord's first gift to him. This likeness was lost through sin; and the contemplative, aware of his sinfulness, turns to her whom the Church hails as 'refuge of sinners'. We may remember that two hundred years after Guigo, an English contemplative, Julian of Norwich, was to say that she had been taught that all who live contemplatively come to union with God by means of Mary. For her, as for Guigo, it was beyond question or controversy that the Mother of God is mediatrix of all graces.

Although the lengthy Meditation VIII is much concerned with the Annunciation, the Incarnation, and their types in the Old Testament, it extends beyond these mysteries to celebrate all Mary's glories, from her own conception, when she was 'separated from the sinful mass of humanity', to her enthronement as Queen of Heaven 'in the nature which is to be raised high above the angels': it hails her as the 'virgin soil' before childbearing, she who in childbearing 'gave birth without anguish' and who after childbearing is still 'unspotted in her virginity'; and, again, it sees in her the perfection of the life of prayer—'you have mounted the six steps of the active life, and upon the seventh, the quiet of contemplation, you enthrone the King of peace'. Much of the typology employed here is traditional, as when Mary is compared with the fleece of Gideon and the tree of life in the 'first good news'; but we must observe that these, and other less common figures from the Old Testament used by Guigo, are found also in Aelred of Rievaulx's *Sermon on the Blessed Virgin Mary.*[88] Other, earlier writers had seen in the great throne of Solomon an image of our Lady. But there are resemblances between the treatment of this in Aelred's sermon and in Guigo so close as to suggest that Aelred is the immediate source. To take one example, Aelred wrote: 'A great throne indeed is that most holy one, for in some fashion she comprehends the incomprehensible, in her womb she enfolds the uncontainable, and what she had contained she preserved';[89] but if we compare this with Guigo—'You are adorned with fine gold of purest wisdom, and as well fashioned in your unspotted virginity as Solomon's throne'—we see that Guigo has not only borrowed, from another place in the same sermon of Aelred, the idea that the gold of the throne signifies Mary's wisdom, but has transferred to this place Aelred's allusion to the throne's capacious solidity as symbolic of her virginity. This may resolve the crux which one editor has observed in 'in her womb' (*sua viscera*):[90] Guigo seems to have used a manuscript with a reading 'in her virginity' (*sua virginitate*), more probably what Aelred wrote. Conversely, this same sermon serves to throw light on an obscure passage in Guigo's Meditation VIII. The present editors have deemed it justifiable to supply their own interpretation of Guigo's *Dominus est, ego ancilla: ille ros, ego terra, inde frumentum: ille manna, ego vas, inde vermiculus,* the last clause of which they have translated 'He is the manna, I the vessel out of which came the scarlet dye, made from the worm,' believing that the cross reference to Leviticus which they have here added explains why Guigo made the 'worm' the type of the incarnate Christ: the scarlet dye signifies the Precious Blood. This conjecture is confirmed by Aelred's sermon: Guigo has

modified Aelred's typology, for he says that the manna
descending from Heaven is Mary, 'whose holiness, containing
in itself all sweetness, flowed down upon us from the
heavens'; but later he adds: 'From this manna is born the
worm, that worm who says in the psalm "I am a worm and
no man," who personifies Him whom David called "the worm
in the wood, wounded beyond all others".' And when Guigo
explains the allusion to the two supporting arms of Solomon's throne by adducing Canticles 2: 6, 'With His left arm
He supports your head . . . ' as a type of God's providence in
preserving Mary's virginity, and says that the throne's seven
steps symbolize 'the six steps of the contemplative life . . .
and the seventh, the quiet of contemplation' which Mary
has attained, he would seem to be following Aelred directly,
rather than any common source. It is Aelred who names the
six previous steps for us: 'Then let each one hasten to mount
to the throne of peace and tranquillity by these six steps,
rejecting the world, despising himself, considering the bonds
of his concupiscent nature which he cannot escape, learning
his own weaknesses, and so let him come by keeping guard
upon his tongue and preserving his body's rest to the peace
of the heart.'

Meditation IX is written in a more affective mood. At
times it has the tone of a sermon preached, at times that of a
marriage song, sung for Mary's 'great feast', 'her royal
nuptials', the Annunciation. The composition of place is
established by oblique reference to earthly marriage feasts,
with their prodigal display of a superabundance of wine
and food, at which not only the bidden guests but the poor
can have their fill, at which there is rejoicing and song.
Naturally, this leads Guigo to meditate upon Christ and
Mary at Cana, where she ensured that there was no lack; but
first we are led to consider Joseph and his careful provision
of plenty in Egypt. Christ, Guigo says, is a second Joseph,
and Mary is his overflowing store from which we are fed;
and we shall sing and rejoice in the sanctuary of God. The

typology here is traditional. Guerric, in his first sermon on the Resurrection, calls Joseph a type of Christ,[91] and Aelred says that Rachel's sterility prefigured the virginity of the mother of our Joseph.[92] But when Aelred treats of the Annunciation as the celebration of Mary's nuptials, there is a certain artificiality, a certain element of the grotesque in his handling of the theme, if we compare it with Guigo's. For Guigo the rejoicing at the feast is the new bridal song of Christ and His Church; and then from consideration of this scene he returns to himself. His spiritual state is symbolized by the lean years in Egypt, by the famine in which the widow in Sarepta was dying; and it is Joseph, Christ, and his store, Mary, who must save him. When the envoys, his brothers, come to him from famine-stricken Canaan, Joseph will eat apart, till in the end he will no longer be able to maintain his disguise, in his excess of love, and will reveal himself to them. Here the double implication, the allusion to our being fed both in the Eucharistic feast and upon the word of God, is plain; and the meditation ends with its highly appropriate quotation from the *Magnificat,* 'He will fill the hungry with good things . . . '.

This implied equation between our receiving God's word and our consuming His body and blood sacramentally, already several times touched on, is dealt with at length in the two Eucharistic meditations, X and XI, which follow; and Meditation X, in particular, shows that many of the ideas and analogies forming the substance of the *Ladder* were already present and active in Guigo's mind, if not yet fully explored. This meditation upon the body of Christ does contain, in places, clear and succinct doctrine upon the Eucharist, but Guigo is not directly concerned with dogma, but with spiritual theology. How, he asks, can we who receive Holy Communion, with complete knowledge that we so consume in our own bodies the body of the Lord, feed upon Him spiritually, to the nourishment and growth of our souls? The purpose of Holy Communion is contemplative union with God. The meditation ends with the admonition that union through faith should lead, as Christ directs, to union in the vision of God; and in treating of the means to this contemplative union, Guigo speaks of Holy Communion precisely as Bernard and his followers speak of contemplative study of the word of God. The effort of receiving and assimilating spiritually the Eucharist is the contemplative effort (the analogy of the processes of mastication and digestion is that which the *Ladder* will apply to the reception of God's word), and the effort will be made through the operation of the spiritual senses under the influence of divine wisdom. In either case, the same contemplative ascesis is called for: The two are inseparably linked, because both are directed to the reception of the same bread of Christ. He has 'lowered the heavens and come down', He has 'condescended to speak in our simple language'; but He has done this so as to bring us by His flesh to the Spirit. (Here we have the substance of the modern theory of 'divine condescension,' and its two-fold application, just as Pius XII in *Divino Afflante* wrote: 'As the substantial word of God became like to man in all things, sin excepted, so the words of God, expressed in human language, became in all things like to human speech, error excepted.') It is meditation that consigns to the memory both the word of God and Christ, who is received in the Eucharist, for the nourishment of the soul. Meditation assimilates and digests. By means of it, what is taken slowly penetrates the understanding. If the understanding is to play its part, meditation, which for Guigo implies also recollection, must be constant. (That Holy Communion will be frequent, probably daily, seems in these Eucharistic meditations to be presupposed.) The memory will so enrich the understanding, and the understanding will strengthen the will to taste this 'solid food'; and at the same time the search in faith will inform the understanding, and lead the soul to that love which is wisdom. Here Guigo is very close to the teaching of one of his masters, William of St. Thierry in

De natura et dignitate amoris, on how love and wisdom together must guide the soul through purgation and initiation to stability.[93]

Meditation XI has also a certain Eucharistic character; but, unlike X, it is essentially eschatological. 'It is for those who have been made perfect to accept this chalice of salvation.' All the previous meditations have been concerned with progress in contemplative prayer, the progress which in the *Ladder* is called the first three rungs of the ladder, mounted by beginners, proficients and devotees. And so here Guigo says that Christ's first seven beatitudes tell how His body is eaten. But the eighth beatitude, 'Blessed are those who suffer persecution', tells how His blood is drunk by the perfect, by the blessed who have attained the fourth and highest rung. To mount so high, to learn to feed upon the body of Christ, is only achieved by long effort and labor. But he uses again the analogy of the physical processes of eating and drinking— ' . . . food has to be chewed . . . but drink is quickly and easily swallowed'—to introduce the statement that 'the sufferings of the perfect are very sweet to them, and seem to pass quickly by'. To drink Christ's chalice with Him is to begin, here and now, to share in the joys of His resurrection. In the passages from Scripture which he uses here, it is the anagogical, mystical sense that predominates. It is the glorified Christ, 'the first born and the prince of all creation', who would have us share the joys of His glory, whose death has changed our cup of bitterness into overflowing sweetness. And as we share this cup with Him we are sealed with His blood and filled with a greater thirst and longing for Him, a longing to bear His sufferings, which transform and fructify our own. We must drink and rejoice, as Scripture tells us: We must drink of the chalice and share Christ's Passion, and we must rejoice to suffer, and in suffering we must find rest and peace, the true Sabbath on which we rest from the work of the senses and rejoice 'in the love of spiritual things'. So suffering will bring the blessedness promised in the eighth beatitude, upon the eighth day, the day of resurrection, Augustine's 'greatest Sabbath' on which God rested after His work of redemption, as all who follow Him must rest.[94] Guigo I, in *Of the Solitary Life,* says that when Christ asked, 'Can you drink of the cup from which I must drink?' He was telling us that we shall only come to the promised banquet if we first drink of the cup of earthly bitterness;[95] Guigo II, with his deep perception of the processes of unitive prayer, tells us in this Meditation XI that in union with God bitterness becomes sweetness, sorrow joy.

It would appear that, apart from X and XI, on the body and blood of the Lord, the *Meditations* were composed separately, in spite of the many links between the first six and the unity of theme in the three meditations on our blessed Lady. At the same time, his constant concern throughout them all is to explore, by means of meditative colloquy either with God or with our Lady as mediatrix, the ways in which he can be guided to the heights of contemplation. The last meditation, in the order presented by R and V, serves as a kind of appendix to X and XI. Here Guigo reconsiders some of the Eucharistic types found in the Old Testament, and gives them further application. He contrasts the fleshly meats for which the Israelites longed, and which signify for him our senses' desires for gratification, with the manna, the bread of angels, with which the Lord fed His people, the true and unchanging food of our souls, the careful, laborious, savoring study of the word of God. In this meditation he uses for his purposes symbols and concepts he found in other men's writing. The author of the *Allegoriae in Sacram Scripturam* says that the quails in the desert stand for carnal pleasure,[96] and that in Psalm 77:27, the 'winged birds like the sand of the sea' signify the transient, perishable created world. When Guigo quotes the Psalmist's 'how sweet are your words in my mouth, sweeter than honey and the honeycomb', that leads him to compare the soul's meditative work with that of the bee, which he calls a 'wise virgin', because, for him and his age, the bee was a symbol of the ascetic life. Eucherius in the *Liber formularum spiritualis intelligentiae* calls the bee the 'form' embodiment of virginity or of wisdom,[97] and the Praemonstratensian abbot, Philip of Harvengt, (†1183) in his life of St. Amandus, explains that a bee flying around the saint's head at Mass was a sign of chastity and of the sweetness of a life of virginity.[98]

In the closing words of Meditation XII, when Guigo says that this bread of angels 'draws man up, back to the place from which he received his likeness', he is reverting to one of the great preoccupations of all the writers of his age concerned with contemplation, to the ideas of 'image theology' which, as we have seen, he has already touched on several times, and which he and his fellows had probably found most clearly expressed in Augustine, as did William of St. Thierry, in the writings of such Greek Fathers as Gregory of Nyssa.[99] Though this meditation may not have been designed to serve as such, it does make a fitting conclusion to the whole collection, and it suggests some of the thoughts which Guigo was to explore more deeply in the *Ladder*. It is far more than a string of pious reflections on the spiritual benefits of Scripture study: It is a closely written summary of his views and findings, as he had so far formulated them, upon the essence of the contemplative life. It is not merely a life of flight and abnegation. It is the world and its pleasures, which the contemplative has renounced, that 'drag down the image of God's glory into the dust', and the restoration of that image must be the goal of the contemplative life. The contemplative is withdrawn, in the desert of the cloister, but if he is to be fed by the bread of angels he must labor, as the children of Israel toiled each day to prepare their heaven-sent manna. It is for this servitude, not for idleness, that he has renounced the works of the world; and if he is to feed upon the food 'containing in itself all sweetness', this will be achieved only by ceaseless effort, the mortification of the body and the exercise of the spirit in the study of the law.

This will bring to him 'every delight and every sweet flavor'; this is the true fruit of contemplation, and so the soul will be restored to the joys and the beauty that fleshly man has dissipated. But we may be sure that when all these meditations had been finished, Guigo had still not achieved that precise analysis of the fourfold nature of the life of contemplation, which he was later to expound in the *Ladder.*

THE MEDITATION ON THE MAGNIFICAT

A meditation on the *Magnificat,* very similar in style to Guigo's *Meditations,* accompanies them in several manuscripts and is also found, independent, in others. Dom H.-M. Rochais describes twelve such texts, and indicates others, more recent, known to him.[100] Of these twelve, Rochais assigns eight to the twelfth century, three to the thirteenth and one to the fourteenth; four of them attribute the work to Bernard, eight are anonymous. In H, the *Magnificat* immediately precedes the *Meditations,* and both are ascribed to Bernard. In P1, the *Magnificat,* unattributed, follows the *Meditations.* In P2 also the *Magnificat* follows the *Meditations,* and both texts are unattributed. In B the *Meditations* precede the *Magnificat,* which is unattributed. In L the *Meditations* and the *Magnificat* are in separate parts of the codex, and they, like all the other contents, are ascribed to Bernard. A printed text called *Sermon on the Canticle of the Blessed Virgin Mary* is in the Mabillon edition of Bernard reproduced by Migne,[101] but the editors question the attribution.

All that the manuscript evidence tells us is that in several early Guigo collections the *Magnificat* is also found. There is no known attribution to Guigo himself. Rochais is inclined to argue for it as a genuine work of Bernard, but his thesis is not wholly convincing. The few striking similarities between phrases and ideas found in the *Magnificat* and in genuine works of Bernard derive mostly from the use of common sources, such as Jerome, *Liber de nominibus hebraicis,* for 'Israel, that is contemplatives', and Gregory, whose 'Love itself is her fame' is quoted both in the *Magnificat* and in Bernard's *De diversis.*

The *Magnificat* is a not especially original treatment of the theme that Mary's glories are best shown in her humility and her free acknowledgment of God's greatness and her own unworthiness. Its manner, certainly, is very much that employed by Guigo in both the *Ladder* and the *Meditations,* depending for its effect upon an ingenious introduction and interweaving of allusions to the Scriptures and the liturgy. Here is a single illustrative example, where the author is speaking of three species of pride—pride of the senses, pride of the intellect and pride in knowledge of hidden mysteries— that are typified by 'the beasts of the field, the birds of the air and the fish who wander the ways of the ocean. These are the fish who burst the nets, those who seek out subtleties, who seem in the eyes of the faithful to be humble little fishes swimming in the water, but who drink not of the sweet waters of the rivers but of the bitter sea: they are sea fish, wandering the ways not of heaven but of the ocean.'

Occasionally the author will broach one of the topics that comes to preoccupy Guigo. So he writes: 'Let not those who fear the Lord despair because of their sins, for "His mercy is upon those who fear Him". His mercy remits the sins of those who fear Him, and the remission of their sins fosters love in those who fear Him,[102] and those who love Him confess His name.' But such places are the merest hints of Guigo's penetrating and affective approach to the study of the psychology of the interior life. The present editors are not convinced that this work is not from the pen of Guigo. But, if it is, we have here a very early and undeveloped work, in no way worthy of comparison with the *Ladder* and the *Meditations;* and it is because of its immaturity and its largely commonplace ideas, rather than because of the dubious attribution to Guigo, that it has not been included in this present edition.

NOTES

Introduction

1. *Auteurs spirituels et textes dévotes de moyen âge latin* (Paris, 1932) p. 217.

2. Ibid. pp. 218-21.

3. *Annales Ordinis Carthusiensis* II (Montreuil, 1888) p. 373.

4. Decima L. Douie and Hugh Farmer, *The Life of St. Hugh of Lincoln I* (London, 1961) p. 45, n. 2.

5. *Annales Ordinis Carthusiensis* II, p. 478.

6. *Ibid.* III, pp. 130-31.

7. *ASS* August IV, 221; W. Heywood: *The 'Ensamples of Fra Filippo'—a Study of Mediaeval Siena* (Siena, 1901) p. 11.

8. Wilmart lists an eighth, Paris, Ste-Geneviève 1367, containing only Meditation VII and VIII: *Auteurs spirituels,* p. 229, n. 1.

9. Dom H. Rochais, in *Enquête sur les sermons divers et les sentences de Saint Bernard* (Analecta S.O.C., Rome XVIII, 1962, Fasc. 3-4) pp. 105-6, lists 12 manuscripts of the meditation on the Magnificat, of the twelfth–thirteenth centuries, and adds that there are several others of more recent date. The only explicit attribution of the work in all these manuscripts is to Bernard or Hugh of St. Victor. Cf. also *Auteurs spirituels,* pp. 228 n. 1 and p. 229 n. 1.

10. *Revue d'ascétique et de mystique 5* (1924) pp. 59-79, 127-58.

11. *Patrologia Latina* (PL) 40:997-1004.

12. PL 184:475-84.

13. *S. Bernardi Opera Omnia I* (1690) Appendix, p. xv.

14. Cf. J. Bulloch, *Adam of Dryburgh* (London, 1958).

15. Ed., Brial, edition of 1869, Vol. 15, p. 11.

16. *Auteurs spirituels,* p. 235 n. 3.

17. *Otia Monastica: Etudes sur le vocabulaire de la contemplation au Moyen Age* (Studia Anselmiana 51, Rome, 1963) p. 129.

18. I. Hausherr, S.J.: *Solitude et vie contemplative d'après l'hésychasme* (Etiolles, 1962) p. 11.

19. *Lettres des premiers Chartreux,* p. 78.

20. *Otia Monastica,* pp. 166-67.

21.   See the valuable article, *Échelle spirituelle,* by Émile Bertaud and André Rayez in the *Dict. de spiritualité,* IV (Paris, 1960) pp. 62–86.

22.   *Expositio in Psalmos,* PL 152:1313; the attribution of this commentary to Bruno is now regarded as uncertain.

23.   *De gradibus caritatis* (PL 196:1195–1208); *De quatuor gradibus violentae caritatis* (ibid., 1207–24).

24.   PL 182:745.

25.   PL 175:116.

26.   V 3; PL 182:790.

27.   PL 175:116.

28.   PL 32:1074, and cf. Guerric of Igny, *Sermon 1;* PL 185:141 [CF 8]; Peter de Celle, *Sermo 69;* PL 202:857; William of St. Thierry, *Epistola Aurea,* X.31; PL 184:327 [CF 12]; *De Sacramento Altaris;* PL 180:352.

29.   *In Matthaei Evangelium Expositio* I 5; PL 92:25. On the authorship of this, see F. Stegmüller: *Repertorium Biblicum Medii Aevi* 2 (Madrid, 1950) no. 1678.

30.   Cf. P. Du Montier, *S. Bernard et la Bible* (Paris, 1953) pp. 110–19.

31.   *Homilia in Ecclesiasten* I; PL 175:117, also used in *De arca Noe morali* III 7; PL 176:654.

32.   PL 180:538. Cf. James Walsh, S.J., *Guillaume de Saint-Thierry et les sens spirituels,* in *Revue d'ascetiqué et de mystique,* 35 (1959) p. 34 and nn. 29, 30, where it is shown that William's first authority is not Bernard but Origen.

33.   5–6, PL 36:466–67.

34.   E.G. Augustine, *De quantiate animae,* 70, 75; PL 32:1073, 1076; and, for a contemporary example, Hugh of St. Victor, *De arca Noe morali* IV 6; PL 176:672.

35.   *Summa Sententiarum* V; PL 176:133. This work is very probably not by Hugh.

36.   PL 180:227.

37.   PL 185:367.

38.   Cf. Hugh of St. Victor, *De Arrha Animae;* PL 176:951–70, and William of St. Thierry, *Orationes Meditativae* XII; PL 180:246.

39.   *Moralia* XV 53; PL 75:1108.

40.   PL 184:386.

41.   PL 38:854.

42.   PL 176:970.

43.   PL 180:215.

44.   PL 176:669.

45.   PL 38:1144. The authorship of this is now disputed, but

E. Dekkers, *Clavis Patrum Latinorum* ([2] Bruges, 1961), does not list it as spurious.

46. Cf. *The Cloud of Unknowing,* ed. William Johnston, S.J. (Garden City, New York: Image Books) pp. 79, 190.

47. PL 184:387.

48. PL 176:636–37.

49. *Magna Vita Sancti Hugonis,* Vol. I, pp. 57, 97–99.

50. *S. Anselmi Opera Omnia,* ed. F. S. Schmitt (Edinburgh, 1956) Vol. III, p. 90.

51. London, 1955, pp. 100–17.

52. Cf. *supra,* p. 10.

53. I[a] II[ae] qu 11a art 1.

54. *Contra Julianum* III 9; PL 44:712.

55. Ibid. VI 19; PL 44:858.

56. I[a] II[ae] qu 113 art 3 ad 2.

57. Sermon 169; PL 38:923.

58. PL 37:1553.

59. PL 45:936.

60. I[a] II[ae] qu 109 art 5.

61. *Auteurs spirituels,* p. 229, n. 1.

62. *Auteurs spirituels,* pp. 218, 226–30.

63. "L'imitation de Jésus-Christ: Méditations inédits de Guigues II le Chartreux," in *Vie Spirituelle,* Supplément, 1932–34.

64. PL 75:706.

65. PL 76:467.

66. PL 153:757–58.

67. PL 153:757–58.

68. PL 153:659.

69. Cf. *Lettres des premiers Chartreux;* SCh 88:142 ff.

70. PL 112:882. Wilmart, however (*Révue Bénédictine,* 1920, pp. 47–56), argues that the *Allegoriae* is the work of Garnier de Rochefort; De Lubac (*Exégèse Médiévale* I, tome I, Paris 1959, p. 152) says that the work belongs to the second half of the twelfth century, and adds that Adam of Dryburgh is probably its author; while Delhaze attributes the work to Godefroy de St. Victor (*Le microcosmus de Godefroy de Saint Victor,* Lille, 1951, pp. 280–81).

71. PL 184:117 [CF 20].

72. PL 202:458.

73. PL 185:196–97.

74. Ibid. 194.

75. *Lettres des premiers Chartreux,* pp. 77–78.

76. Sermo II, In Dominica Palmarum; PL 185:132–33.

77. Max Bonnet, *Acta Andreae* (Paris, 1855) p. 69.

78.   One of St. Bernard's companions at Clairvaux, Nicholas, in a sermon for the feast of St. Andrew, speaks of seven steps in the ascent to the knowledge of God. The seventh, he says, is perseverance, *perseverantia bonitatis;* and he adds: "and in this seventh grade the Lord will call you, with Moses, out of the midst of the cloud; and you will fix your interior gaze on the very substance of God" (PL 184:1053-54). St. Bernard himself alludes also to the legend of St. Andrew who prayed "that he might not be taken down from the cross" (Sermo II *in festo St. Andreae;* PL 182:514).

79.   PL 189:1518-19.

80.   Cf. *Vetus Latina: die Reste der altlateinischen Bibel,* ed. B. Fischer, O.S.B. (Freiburg, 1951-54).

81.   PL 152:816.

82.   PL 176:668-69.

83.   *Tractatus XLIX, caput XL, 3;* PL 35:1747-48.

84.   PL 189:1519-20.

85.   "Le monachisme clunisien", in *Théologie de la vie monastique* (Lyons, 1961).

86.   PL 14:452.

87.   PL 195:253-54.

88.   *Sermones Inediti B. Aelredi Abbatis Rievallensis,* ed. C. H. Talbot (Rome, 1952), pp. 136-44. There are elements common both to Aelred and Guigo in *Allegoriae in Vetus Testamentum* (e.g. VII c. V *De throno Solomonis,* and c. XI *De Elia et vidua Sareptana*), attributed in Migne (PL 175, 706-9) to Hugh of St. Victor. But according to J. Chatillon (*Révue du moyen âge latin,* 1948, pp. 23-52), the work is Richard of St. Victor's *Liber exceptionum.*

89.   *Sermones,* p. 137.

90.   *Aelred de Rievaulx, Sermons inédits,* (Mariale II, Pain de Citeaux 6, 1960) p. 66.

91.   PL 185:141 ff.

92.   PL 195:253.

93.   PL 184:381.

94.   PL 34:33; PL 38, 1090.

95.   *Lettres des premiers chartreux,* pp. 144-46.

96.   PL 112:904.

97.   PL 50:751.

98.   PL 203:1254-55.

99.   It should be noticed that the works of Origen and Gregory of Nyssa would have been available to Guigo in Latin translation, as the surviving manuscripts of the library of the Grande Chartreuse in the twelfth century testify.

100. *Analecta S.O.C.,* Rome, XVIII, 1962, Fasc. 3–4, pp. 105–6.
101. PL 184:1121–28.
102. Or, in other manuscripts, "in those who know Him."

THE LADDER OF MONKS

A Letter on the Contemplative Life

I. PROLOGUE

BROTHER GUIGO to his dear brother
Gervase: rejoice in the Lord. I owe you a debt
of love, brother, because you began to love
me first;* and since in your previous letter
you have invited me to write to you, I feel
bound to reply. So I decided to send you my
thoughts on the spiritual exercises proper to
cloistered monks, so that you who have come
to know more about these matters by your
experience than I have by theorizing about
them may pass judgment on my thoughts*
and amend them. And it is fitting that I
should offer these first results of our work
together to you before anyone else, so that
you may gather the first fruits of the young
tree* which by praiseworthy stealth you extracted from the bondage of Pharaoh,* where
it was tended alone, and set it in its place
among the ordered rows,* once you had
grafted on to the stock like a good nursery-
man the branch skillfully cut from the
wild olive.*

Cf. 1 Jn 4:10

Cf. Heb 4:12

Cf. Ps 143:12
Cf. Ex 13:14

Cf. Sg 6:3, 9

Cf. Rom 11:17,24

II. THE FOUR RUNGS OF THE LADDER

One day when I was busy working with my
hands I began to think about our spiritual
work, and all at once four stages in spiritual

exercise came into my mind: reading, meditation, prayer and contemplation. These make a
ladder for monks by which they are lifted up
from earth to heaven. It has few rungs, yet its
length is immense and wonderful, for its lower

Sir 35:21   end rests upon the earth, but its top pierces
†*Cf. Gen 28:12*   the clouds* and touches heavenly secrets.†
Just as its rungs or degrees have different
names and numbers, they differ also in order
and quality; and if anyone inquires carefully
into their properties and functions, what each
one does in relation to us, the differences
between them and their order of importance,
he will consider whatever trouble and care he
may spend on this little and easy in comparison with the help and consolation which

Cf. Gen 29:20   he gains.*

Reading is the careful study of the Scriptures, concentrating all one's powers on it.
Meditation is the busy application of the
mind to seek with the help of one's own
reason for knowledge of hidden truth. Prayer
is the heart's devoted turning to God to drive
away evil and obtain what is good. Contemplation is when the mind is in some sort lifted
up to God and held above itself, so that it
tastes the joys of everlasting sweetness. Now
that we have described the four degrees, we
must see what their functions are in relation to us.

III. THE FUNCTIONS OF THESE DEGREES

Reading seeks for the sweetness of a blessed
life, meditation perceives it, prayer asks for it,

contemplation tastes it. Reading, as it were, puts food whole into the mouth,* meditation chews it and breaks it up, prayer extracts its flavor, contemplation is the sweetness itself which gladdens and refreshes. Reading works on the outside, meditation on the pith:* prayer asks for what we long for, contemplation gives us delight in the sweetness which we have found. To make this clearer, let us take one of many possible examples.

Cf. 1 Cor 3:2, Heb 5:12;

Cf. Ps 80:17; 147:14

IV. THE FUNCTION OF READING

I hear the words read: 'Blessed are the pure in heart, for they shall see God'.* This is a short text of Scripture, but it is of great sweetness, like a grape that is put into the mouth filled with many senses to feed the soul. When the soul has carefully examined it, it says to itself, There may be something good here. I shall return to my heart* and try to understand and find this purity, for this is indeed a precious and desirable thing. Those who have it are called blessed. It has for its reward the vision of God which is eternal life, and it is praised in so many places in sacred Scripture. So, wishing to have a fuller understanding of this, the soul begins to bite and chew upon this grape, as though putting it in a wine press, while it stirs up its power of reasoning to ask what this precious purity may be and how it may be had.

Cf. Mt 5:8

Cf. Lk 15:18

V. THE FUNCTION OF MEDITATION

When meditation busily applies itself to this work, it does not remain on the outside, is not detained by unimportant things, climbs higher, goes to the heart of the matter, examines each point thoroughly. It takes careful note that the text does not say: 'Blessed are the pure in body', but 'the pure in heart', for it is not enough to have hands clean from evil deeds,* unless our minds are cleansed from impure thoughts. We have the authority of the prophet for this, when he says: 'Who shall climb the mountain of the Lord, and who shall stand in His holy place? He whose hands are guiltless and whose heart is pure.'* And meditation perceives how greatly that same prophet seeks for this purity of heart when he prays: 'Create a pure heart in me, God',* and in another place: 'If I know that there is wickedness in my heart, the Lord will not hear me'.* It thinks what care the saintly man Job took to preserve this purity; when he said: 'I have made a pact with my eyes, so that I would not think about any maid.'* See how this holy man guarded himself, who shut his eyes lest he should look upon vain things,* lest he should perhaps unguardedly see that which afterward he should long for despite himself.

After meditation has so pondered upon purity of heart, it begins to think of the reward, of how glorious and joyful it would be to see the face of the Lord so greatly longed for,* 'fairer than all the sons of men',* no longer rejected and wretched,† not

Cf. Gen 37:22

Ps 23:3-4

Ps 50:10

Ps 65:18

Job 31:1

Cf. Ps 118:37

Cf. Ps 26:8
Ps 44:3.
†Cf. Is 53:2

with that earthly beauty with which His
mother clothed Him, but wearing the robe of
immortality and crowned with the diadem* *Cf. Is 53:2*
which His Father bestowed upon Him on the
day of His resurrection and glory,* the day *Cf. Sir 6:32*
'which the Lord has made'.* It thinks how *Ps 17:24*
this vision will bring it the fullness of which
the prophet says: 'I shall be filled when your
glory appears.'* Do you see how much juice *Ps 16:15*
has come from one little grape, how great a
fire has been kindled from a spark,* how this *Cf. Sir 11:34*
small piece of metal, 'Blessed are the pure in
heart, for they shall see God', has acquired a
new dimension by being hammered out on the
anvil of meditation? And even more might be
drawn from it at the hands of someone truly
expert. I feel that 'the well is deep', but I am
still an ignorant beginner, and it is only with
difficulty that I have found something in
which to draw up these few drops.* When the *Jn 4:11*
soul is set alight by this kindling, and when its
flames are fanned by these desires, it receives
a first intimation of the sweetness, not yet by
tasting but through its sense of smell, when
the alabaster box is broken;* and from this it *Cf. Mk 14:3*
deduces how sweet it would be* to know by *Cf. Ps 33:9*
experience the purity that meditation has
shown to be so full of joy.

But what is it to do? It is consumed with
longing, yet it can find no means of its own
to have what it longs for; and the more it
searches the more it thirsts. As long as it is
meditating, so long is it suffering,* because it *Cf. Qo 1:18*
does not feel that sweetness which, as medita-
tion shows, belongs to purity of heart, but
which it does not give. A man will not

experience this sweetness while reading or
meditating 'unless it happened to be given
him from above'.* The good and the wicked
alike can read and meditate; and even pagan
philosophers by the use of reason discovered
the highest and truest good. But 'although
they knew God, they did not glorify Him as
God',* and trusting in their own powers they
said: 'Let us sing our own praises, our words
are our own.'* They had not the grace to
understand what they had the ability to see.
'They perished in their own ideas',* and 'all
their wisdom was swallowed up',* that wisdom to which the study of human learning
had led them, not the Spirit of wisdom who
alone grants true wisdom,* that sweet-tasting
knowledge that rejoices and refreshes the
soul in which it dwells with a sweetness beyond telling. Of this wisdom it is said: 'Wisdom will not enter a disaffected soul.'* This
wisdom comes only from God; and just as
the Lord entrusted the office of baptizing to
many, but reserved to Himself alone the
power and the authority truly to remit sins in
baptism, so that John called Him by His office
and defined it when he said: 'This is He who
baptizes',* so we may say of Him: 'This is He
who gives the sweetness of wisdom and makes
knowledge sweet to the soul. He gives words
to many, but to few that wisdom of the soul
which the Lord apportions to whom He
pleases and when He pleases.*

Jn 19:11

Rom 1:21

Ps 11:5

Rom 1:21
Ps 106:27

Cf. Jm 1:17

Wis 1:4

Jn 1:33

1 Cor 12:11

VI. THE FUNCTION OF PRAYER

So the soul, seeing that it cannot attain by

itself to that sweetness of knowing and
feeling for which it longs, and that the more
'the heart abases itself',* the more 'God is   *Ps 63:7*
exalted',* humbles itself and betakes itself to   *Ps 63:8*
prayer, saying: Lord, you are not seen except
by the pure of heart. I seek by reading and
meditating what is true purity of heart and
how it may be had, so that with its help I may
know you, if only a little. Lord, for long have
have I meditated in my heart,* seeking to see   *Cf. Ps 76:7*
your face.* It is the sight of you, Lord, that I   *Cf. Ps 26:8*
have sought; and all the while in my medita-
tion the fire of longing,* the desire to know   *Cf. Ps 38:4*
you more fully, has increased. When you
break for me the bread of sacred Scripture,*   *Cf. Lk 24:30-31*
you have shown yourself to me in that break-
ing of bread,* and the more I see you, the   *Cf. Lk 24:35*
more I long to see you, no more from with-
out, in the rind of the letter, but within, in
the letter's hidden meaning. Nor do I ask this,
Lord, because of my own merits, but because
of your mercy. I too in my unworthiness confess my sins with the woman who said that
'even the little dogs eat of the fragments that
fall from the table of their masters'.* So give   *Mt 15:27*
me, Lord, some pledge of what I hope to
inherit, at least one drop of heavenly rain with
which to refresh my thirst,* for I am on fire   *Cf. Lk 16:24*
with love.   *Cf. Sg 2:5*

VII. THE EFFECTS OF CONTEMPLATION

So the soul by such burning words inflames
its own desire, makes known its state, and by
such spells it seeks to call its spouse. But the

Cf. Ps 33:16;
1 Pet 3:12.

Lord, whose eyes are upon the just and whose
ears can catch not only the words,* but the
very meaning of their prayers, does not wait
until the longing soul has said all its say,
but breaks in upon the middle of its prayer,
runs to meet it in all haste, sprinkled with
sweet heavenly dew, anointed with the most
precious perfumes, and He restores the weary
soul, He slakes its thirst, He feeds its hunger,
He makes the soul forget all earthly things:
by making it die to itself He gives it new life
in a wonderful way, and by making it drunk
He brings it back to its true senses. And just
as in the performance of some bodily functions the soul is so conquered by carnal
desire that it loses all use of the reason, and
man becomes as it were wholly carnal, so on
the contrary in this exalted contemplation all
carnal motives are so conquered and drawn
out of the soul that in no way is the flesh
opposed to the spirit, and man becomes, as it
were, wholly spiritual.

VIII. THE SIGNS OF THE COMING
OF GRACE

But, Lord, how are we to know when you
do this, what will be the sign of your
coming?* Can it be that the heralds and witnesses of this consolation and joy are sighs
and tears? If it is so, then the word consolation is being used in a completely new sense,
the reverse of its ordinary connotation. What
has consolation in common with sighs, joy
with tears, if indeed these are to be called

Cf. Mt 24:3

tears and not rather an abundance of spiritual
dew, poured out from above and overflowing, an outward purification as a sign of inward cleansing. For just as in the baptism of
infants by the outward washing, the inward
cleansing is typified and shown, here conversely an outward washing proceeds from
the inner cleansing. These are blessed tears,
by which our inward stains are cleansed, by
which the fires of our sins are put out.
'Blessed are they who weep' so, 'for they
shall rejoice.'* When you weep so, O my   *Mt 5:5*
soul, recognize your spouse, embrace Him
whom you long for, make yourself drunk
with this torrent of delight,* and suck the   *Cf. Ps 35:8*
honey and milk of consolation from the
breast.* The wonderful reward and comforts   *Cf. Is 66:11*
which your spouse has brought and awarded
you are sobbings and tears. These tears are
the generous draught which He gives you to
drink.* Let these tears be your bread by day   *Cf. Ps 79:6*
and night,* the bread which strengthens the   *Cf. Ps 41:4*
heart of man,* sweeter than honey and the   *Cf. Ps 103:15*
honeycomb.* O Lord Jesus, if these tears,   *Cf. Ps 18:11*
provoked by thinking of you and longing for
you, are so sweet, how sweet will be the joy
which we shall have to see you face to face?
(If it is so sweet to weep for you, how sweet
will it be to rejoice in you?) But why do we
give this public utterance to what should be
said in secret? (Why do we try to express in
everyday languate affections that no language
can describe?) Those who have not known
such things do not understand them, for they
could learn more clearly of them only from
the book of experience where God's grace

Cf. 1 Jn 2:27

hermeneutics

itself is the teacher.* Otherwise it is of no
use for the reader to search in earthly books:
(there is little sweetness in the study of the
literal sense, unless there be a commentary,
which is found in the heart, to reveal the
inward sense.)

IX. HOW GRACE IS HIDDEN

O my soul, we have talked like this too
long. Yet it would have been good for us to
be here, to look with Peter and with John
upon the glory of the spouse and to remain
awhile with Him, had it been His will that we
should make here not two, not three taber-

Cf. Mt 17:4

nacles,* but one in which we might all dwell
and be filled with joy. But now, the spouse
says, 'Let me go, for now the dawn is coming

Gen 32:26

up',* now you have received the light of
grace and the visitation which you asked for.
So He gives His blessing, and withers the
nerve of the thigh, and changes Jacob's name

Cf. Gen 32:25-32

to Israel,* and then for a little while He withdraws, this spouse waited for so long, so soon
gone again. He goes, it is true, for this visitation ends, and with it the sweetness of contemplation; but yet He stays, for He directs
us, He gives us grace, He joins us to Himself.

X. HOW, WHEN GRACE IS HIDDEN
FOR A TIME, IT WORKS IN US FOR GOOD

But do not fear, bride of the spouse, do not
despair, do not think yourself despised, if for

a little while He turns His face away from you. These things all work together for your good,* and you profit from His coming and from His withdrawal. He comes to you, and then He goes away again. He comes for your consolation, He goes away to put you on your guard, for fear that too much consolation should puff you up,* and that you having the spouse always with you, should begin to despise your brethren, and to attribute this consolation not to His grace but to your natural powers. For this grace the spouse bestows when He pleases and to whom He pleases; it is not possessed as though by lawful title. There is a common saying that too much familiarity breeds contempt. And so He withdraws Himself, so that He is not despised for being too attentive, so that when He is absent He may be desired the more, that being desired He may be sought more eagerly, that having been sought for He may at last be found with greater thankfulness.

    Then, too, if we never lacked this consolation, which is a mere shadow and fraction* in comparison with the future glory that will be shown in us,* we might think that we have here on earth our eternal home, and so we should seek the less for our life in eternity.* So, therefore, lest we should consider this present exile our true home, this pledge our whole reward, the spouse comes and withdraws by turn, now bringing us consolation, now exchanging all this for weakness.* For a short time He allows us to taste how sweet He is,* and before our taste is satisfied He withdraws; and it is in this way, by flying

Cf. Rom 8:28

Cf. 2 Cor 12:7

Cf. 2 Cor 13:12

Cf. Rom 8:18

Cf. Heb 13:14

Cf. Ps 40:4

Cf. Ps 33:9

above us with wings outspread, that He en-
Cf. Deut 32:11   courages us to fly,* and says in effect: See
now, you have had a little taste of how sweet
Cf. 1 Pet 2:3   and delightful I am,* but if you wish to have
your fill of this sweetness, hasten after me,
Cf. Sg 1:3   drawn by my sweet-smelling perfumes,* lift
up your heart to where I am at the right hand
Cf. Acts 7:55   of God the Father.* There you will see
Jn 16:19   me* not darkly in a mirror but face to
1 Cor 13:12   face,* and 'your heart's joy will be complete
and no one shall take this joy away from
Jn 16:22   you'.*

XI. HOW MUCH THE SOUL MUST BE
ON ITS GUARD AFTER IT HAS BEEN
VISITED BY GRACE

But take care, bride of the spouse. When
He goes away, He does not go far; and even if
you cannot see Him, you are always in His
Cf. Ezek 1:18   sight. He is full of eyes in front and behind,*
you cannot hide from Him anywhere, for He
surrounds you with those messengers of His,
spirits who serve to bring back shrewd reports,
to watch how you behave when He is not
there, to accuse you to Him if they detect in
you any marks of wantonness and vileness.
Cf Ex 34:14   This is a jealous spouse.* He will leave you at
once and give His favors to others if you play
Him false with anyone, trying to please any-
more than Him. This spouse is fastidious, He
is of gentle birth, He is rich, 'He is fairer
Ps 44:3   than all the sons of men,'* and so He will not
deign to take a bride who is not fair. If He
Cf. Eph 5:27   sees in you any blemish, any wrinkle,* He

will at once turn away from you.* He cannot
bear uncleanness of any kind. So be chaste,
be truly modest and meek, if you wish often
to enjoy your spouse's company.

Cf. Is 1:15

I am afraid that I have talked too long of
this to you, but I have been compelled to it
by the abundance and the sweetness of my
material. I have not deliberately drawn it out,
but its very sweetness has drawn it out of me
against my will.

XII. RECAPITULATION

Let us now gather together by way of
summary what we have already said at length,
so that we may have a better view by looking
at it altogether. You can see, from what has
already been said by way of examples, how
these degrees are joined to each other. One
precedes another, not only in the order of
time but of causality. Reading comes first,
and is, as it were, the foundation; it provides
the subject matter we must use for meditation. Meditation considers more carefully
what is to be sought after; it digs,* as it were,
for treasure which it finds* and reveals, but
since it is not in meditation's power to seize
upon the treasure, it directs us to prayer.
Prayer lifts itself up to God with all its
strength, and begs for the treasure it longs
for, which is the sweetness of contemplation.
Contemplation when it comes rewards the
labors of the other three; it inebriates the
thirsting soul with the dew of heavenly sweetness. Reading is an exercise of the outward

Cf. Pr 2:4
Cf. Mt 13:44

senses; meditation is concerned with the
inward understanding; prayer is concerned
with desire; contemplation outstrips every
faculty. The first degree is proper to beginners, the second to proficients, the third to
devotees, the fourth to the blessed.

XIII. HOW THESE DEGREES ARE LINKED
ONE TO ANOTHER

At the same time these degrees are so linked
together, each one working also for the
others, that the first degrees are of little or no
use without the last, while the last can never,
or hardly ever, be won without the first. For
what is the use of spending one's time in con-
tinuous reading, turning the pages of the lives
and sayings of holy men, unless we can extract nourishment from them by chewing and
digesting this food so that its strength can
pass into our inmost heart? It is only thus
that we can from their example carefully
consider our state of soul, and reflect in our
own deeds the lives about which we read so
eagerly. But how is it possible to think properly, and to avoid meditating upon false
and idle topics, overstepping the bounds laid
down by our holy fathers,* unless we are first
directed in these matters by what we read or
what we hear? Listening is a kind of reading,
and that is why we are accustomed to say that
we have read not only those books which we
have read to ourselves or aloud to others but
those also which our teachers have read to us.

Again, what use is it to anyone if he sees in

Cf. Pr 22:28

his meditation what is to be done, unless the help of prayer and the grace of God enable him to achieve it? For 'every gift and every perfect gift is from above, coming down from the Father of lights'.* We can do nothing without Him. It is He who achieves our works in us, and yet not entirely without us. 'For we are God's fellow workers',* as the apostle says. It is God's will, then, that we pray to Him, His will that when His grace comes and knocks at our door,* we should willingly open our hearts to Him and give Him our consent.

Jm 1:17

1 Cor 3:9

Cf. Rev 3:20

It was this consent that He demanded from the Samaritan woman when He said: 'Call your husband.'* It was as if He said: 'I want to fill you with grace, and you must exercise your free choice.' He demanded prayer from her: 'If you only knew the gift of God, and who He is who says to you, Give me drink, you would perhaps ask Him for living waters.'* When the woman heard this, it was as if the Lord had read it to her, and she meditated on this instruction in her heart, thinking that it would be good and useful for her to have this water. Fired with the desire for it, she had recourse to prayer, saying: 'Lord, give me this water, that I may thirst no more'.* You can see that it was because she had heard the Lord's word and then had meditated on it that she was moved to prayer. How could she have pressed her petition, had she not first been fired by meditation? What profit would her meditation have been, if the prayer that followed had not asked for what she had been shown she should desire? From this we

Jn 4:16

Jn 4:10

Jn 4:15

learn that if meditation is to be fruitful, it
must be followed by devoted prayer, and the
sweetness of contemplation may be called the
effect of prayer.

XIV. SOME CONCLUSIONS FROM
WHAT HAS BEEN SAID

From this we may gather that reading
without meditation is sterile, meditation without reading is liable to error, prayer without
meditation is lukewarm, meditation without
prayer is unfruitful, prayer when it is fervent
wins contemplation, but to obtain it without
prayer would be rare, even miraculous. However, there is no limit to God's power and His
merciful love surpasses all His other works;
and sometimes He creates sons for Abraham
Cf. Mt 3:9   from the very stones,* when He forces the
hard-hearted and reluctant to comply of their
own free will. He acts like a prodigal father, or
as the proverb has it, He gives the ox by the
horn, when He enters where He has not been
invited, when He dwells in the soul that has
not sought Him. Although we are told that
Acts 9   this has occasionally happened to St. Paul,*
for instance, and certain others, we ought not
to presume that it will, for this would be like
tempting God. Rather we should do our part,
which is to read and meditate on the law of
God, and pray to Him to help our weak-
Cf. Rom 8:26   ness* and to look kindly on our infirmities.
He teaches us to do this when He says:
'Ask and you will receive, seek and you will
find, knock and the door will be opened to

you.'* For then 'the kingdom of heaven sub-   *Mt 7:7*
mits to force, and the forceful take it by
storm'.*   *Mt 11:12*

From these definitions you can see how the
various qualities of these degrees are linked
one with another, and the effects which each
one produces in us. Blessed is the man whose
heart is not possessed by any other concern
and whose desire is always to keep his feet
upon this ladder. He has sold all his possessions, and has bought the field in which lies
hid the longed-for treasure.* He wants to be   *Cf. Mt 13:44*
free from all else, and to see how sweet the
Lord is.* The man who has worked in this   *Cf. Ps 33:9, 45:11*
first degree, who has pondered well in the
second, who has known devotion in the third,
who has been raised above himself in the
fourth, goes from strength to strength by
this ascent on which his whole heart was set,
until at last he can see the God of gods in
Sion.* Blessed is the man to whom it is given   *Cf. Ps 83:8*
to remain, if only for a short time, in this
highest degree. In truth he can say: 'Now
indeed I experience God's grace, now with
Peter and John upon the mountain I gaze
upon his glory, now with Jacob I delight in
the embraces of the lovely Rachel.'

But let such a man beware lest after this
contemplation, in which he was lifted up to
the very heavens, he plunged violently into the
depths, and after such great graces turn again
to the sinful pleasures of the world and the
delights of the flesh. Since, however, the eye
of the human heart has not the power to bear
for long the shining of the true light, let the
soul descend gently and in due order to one or

other of the three degrees by means of which
it made its ascent. Let it rest now in one, now
in another, as the circumstances of time and
place suggest to its free choice, even though,
as it seems to me, the soul is the nearer to
God the farther it climbs from the first degree. Such, alas, is the frailty and wretchedness of human nature!

In this way, then, we see clearly by reason
and the testimony of the Scriptures that the
perfection of the blessed life is contained in
these four degrees, and that the spiritual man
ought to occupy himself in them continually.
But is there anyone who holds to this way of
life? 'Tell us who he is and we will praise
him.'* There are many who desire it, but
few who achieve it.* Would that we were
among these few!

Sir 31:9

Cf. Rom 7:18

XV. FOUR OBSTACLES TO THESE DEGREES

There are commonly four obstacles to
these three degrees: unavoidable necessity,
the good works of the active life, human
frailty, worldly follies. The first can be ex-
cused, the second endured, the third invites
compassion, the fourth blame. Blame truly,
for it would be better for the man who for
love of the world turns his back on the goal if
he had never known God's grace, rather than,
having known it, to retrace his steps. For what
excuse will he find for his sin?* Will not the
Lord justly say to him: 'What more should I
have done for you that I have not done?*
When you did not exist I created you, when

Cf. Jn 15:22

Cf. Is 5:4

you sinned and became the devil's slave I re-
deemed you, when you were going about with
the wicked of this world* I called you
away.* I let you find favor in my sight, I
wanted to make my dwelling with you,* and
you gave me nothing but contempt. It was not
my words alone that you repudiated, it was
my own self,* and instead you turned away
in pursuit of your desires.'*

But O my God, so good so tender and kind,
dear friend, wise counsellor, powerful support, how heartless and how rash is the man
who rejects you, who casts from his heart so
humble and gentle a guest! What a wretched
and ruinous bargain, to accept evil and harm-
ful thoughts in exchange for his creator, so
quickly to throw open the inner chamber of
the Holy Spirit, that secret place of the heart
which so recently echoed with heavenly joys,
to unclean thoughts, to turn it into a pig sty.*
Adulterous desires press in upon the heart
where the footprints of the spouse are still
plain to be seen. How ill it accords, how
unseemly it is, for ears which so recently
listened to words which man may not utter,*
so quickly to attend to idle and slanderous
stories,* for eyes so newly purified by holy
tears to turn their gaze so soon on worldly
vanities, for the tongue which has scarcely
ended its sweet song of welcome to the
spouse, scarcely has made peace between Him
and the bride with its burning and pleading
eloquence, and has greeted her in the ban-
queting hall,* to revert to foul talk, to
scurrility, to lampoons and libels. Never let
this happen to us, Lord, and even if we do so

Cf. Ps 11:9
Cf. Is 43:7-11
Cf. Jn 14:23

Cf. Ps 49:17
Cf. Sir 18:30

Cf. Mt 7:6

Cf. 2 Cor 12:4

Cf. 2 Tm 4:4

Cf. Sg 2:4

fall away through human frailty, never let us
despair on that account, but let us hasten
back to the merciful healer who lifts up the
helpless ones out of the dust, and rescues the
Ps 112:7 poor and wretched from the mire;* for He
Cf. Ezek 33:11 who never desires the death of a sinner* will
Cf. Hos 6:2 tend us and heal us again and again.

    Now it is time for us to end our letter. Let
us beseech the Lord together that at this
moment He will lighten the load that weighs
us down so that we cannot look up to Him in
contemplation, and in days to come remove it
altogether, leading us through these degrees
from strength to strength, until we come to
Cf. Ps 83:8 look upon the God of gods in Sion,* where
His chosen enjoy the sweetness of divine
contemplation, not drop by drop, not now
and then, but in an unceasing flow of delight
Cf. Jn 16:22 which no one shall take away,* an unchang-
Cf. Ps 4:9 ing peace, the peace of God.*

    So, my brother Gervase, if it is ever granted
to you from above to climb to the topmost
rung of this ladder, when this happiness is
yours, remember me and pray for me. So,
Cf. Ex 26 when the veil* between you and God is
drawn aside, may I too see Him, 'and may He
Rv 22:17 who listens say to me also: Come.'*

TWELVE MEDITATIONS

'It is good for me, Lord, that you have
humbled me, so that I might learn your true
ways.'* 'It is good for a man to have borne   *Ps 118:71*
your burden since he was young; let him sit
alone and be silent.'* Yet how can anyone be   *Lam 3:27-8*
alone, Lord God of hosts, who is with you?
'But', you say, 'I am not alone; for he who
sent me is with me, the Father.'* Lord Jesus,   *Jn 8:16*
please explain this extraordinary thing you
appear to be saying. You were, it seems, on
familiar terms with men; you ate and drank
with them, and talked to the crowds; and you
remind us that you were not alone: 'I am not
alone', you say, 'for he who sent me is with
me, the Father.' I do not mean those who are
outside me; but I mean who is with me
within. Outwardly, he whose treacherous
hand is with mine in the dish is with me; but
inwardly he is against me, making a pact with
the enemy. Outwardly, he eats my bread;
inwardly, he is counting his money. Out-   *Cf. Mt 26:23,*
wardly, he offers me a kiss, inwardly poison.*   *26:49*

'He who is not with me is against me',* and   *Mt 12:30*
he who is against me is far away from me. My
good Jesus, my desire is that no one should be
with me outwardly, that inwardly I might be
your friend. 'Woe to the lonely man'* when   *Qo 4:10*
you alone are not with him. How many in a
crowd are alone because you are not with

89

them? Be always with me, so that I may never
be alone! I am in no man's company, and yet
I am not alone. I myself am a crowd. My wild
beasts are with me, those whom I have
nourished in my heart from my childhood.
There they have made their lairs which they
love so much that even in my loneliness they
will not leave me. How often have I pro-
tested to them: 'Go away from me, wicked
ones, so that I may search out the commandments of my God.'* It is as though frogs
were croaking in my entrails,* as if Egypt's
plague of flies were binding my eyes.*

Ps 118:115

Cf. Ps 104:30

Cf. Ex 8:21-31

Let him sit alone, the Scripture says; and
indeed, unless he sits and rests, he will not be
alone. So it is good to be humbled, Lord, and
to bear your burden. By carrying your burden
the proud learn meekness. And you say to
those who take up your burden: 'Learn from
me, for I am meek and humble of heart.'* He
who is mounted on pride does not know how
to sit still. But your throne is humility and
peace. And now I see that no one can be at
peace until he has become humble. Humility
and peace: how good it is for a man to be
humbled so that he can attain to peace. Then
indeed will he sit alone and be silent. He who
is not alone cannot be silent. And he who is
not silent cannot hear you when you speak to
him. The Scripture says: 'the words of the
wise are as a goad'* to those who listen to
them in silence. Let all my world be silent in
your presence, Lord,* so that I may hear what
the Lord God may say in my heart.* Your
words are so softly spoken* that no one can
hear them except in a deep silence. But to

Mt 11:29

Qo 12:11

Cf. I Macc 1:3

Ps 84:9

Cf. Job 4:12

hear them lifts him who sits alone and in silence completely above his natural powers, because he who humbles himself will be lifted up.* He who sits alone and listens will   *Lk 14:11* be raised above himself. But where? This surely does not mean a lifting up of the body? No: It means of the heart. But how can his heart be above himself? It can because he forgets himself, does not love himself, thinks nothing of himself. Of what then does he think? Of that which is above him, his highest good, his God. And the more he sees and loves God, the more he sees and loves himself.

II

Speak, Lord, to the heart of your servant, so
that my heart may speak to you; speak to
this orphan, abandoned by all but you. 'The
poor man has abandoned himself to you, to
the destitute you will be a helper.' You have
separated my friend and my dear one from
me;* but you will not separate me from your
help.'* 'My brothers withdrew themselves
from me as though they were strangers';* but
'do not withdraw yourself, Lord from me.'*
'Those whom I knew you have sent far away
from me; they treat me as one who defiles
them;* they have opened their mouths against
me,* and they have cursed my soul.' Do not
make them responsible for this, 'for they
think that they are offering service to God.'*
They may curse me, but you will bless* both
them and me. 'For you are the Lord of hosts,
who judge justly and see down into the
depths of men's hearts.'* 'I have shown you
how it is with me',* defender of my life. And
now, Lord, 'there is no one to help me';*
there is no man near me to console and aid
me. 'My soul rejected all other consolation*
so that your solace might rejoice my soul.'*
'My eyes were upon you that you might free
me from this maze.'* 'But my eyes grew
heavy as I waited for your promised word of
consolation.'*

Ps 9:14

Ps 87:19
Ps 21:20
Job 19:13
Ps 34:22

Ps 87:9
Ps 21:14

Jn 16:2
Ps 108:28

Jer 11:20
Jer 20:12
Job 6:13

Ps 76:3
Ps 93:19

Ps 24:15

Ps 118:82

I remember how Anna stood at the gate of your sanctuary, weeping bitterly, and how her husband Helcana, sorrowing because of her sorrow, sought to console her whom he loved: 'Anna, why do you weep? Why will you not eat? Am I not more to you than ten sons?'* Still she wept and would not eat, for the only bread which pleased her was 'the bread of tears'.* She refused human consolation,* preferring the joy of the Lord her God, as he did who said: 'Lord, you know that I have not longed for man's delights.'* So she wept and did not eat. 'Blessed are they who mourn, for they will be comforted.'* The tears on the widow's cheeks go up to you;* you, who hear her, take no delight in her sorrow.

Cf. 1 Kgs 1

Ps 79:6
Cf. Ps 76:3

Jer 17:16

Mt 5:5
Cf. Sir 35:18-19

So there is nothing better that I can do than to weep, as did Jeptha's daughter, for the barrenness of my soul.* 'My soul is barren, Lord',* and so I fear lest I be cursed according to your law: the woman accursed and barren bears no child. Such a curse must be feared. Because of this barrenness Anna wept and did not eat. But 'you looked upon her tears',* and she conceived and bore a son, whom she consecrated to your service.

Cf. Judg 11
Cf. Num 11:6; Ps 34:12

Ps 55:9

A soil is rich when it is watered with tears, and brings forth fruit a hundredfold. 'Send down your rain, Lord, from on high'* that 'the earth may receive it and produce the the fruit of salvation',* so that the hungry may be filled, and the barren bear sevenfold.* 'This is the generation of those who seek the Lord, who seek the face of the God of Jacob.'* Let this generation be blessed for

Ps 103:13

Is 45:8
Cf. 1 Kgs 2:5

Ps 23:6

ever. For the sake of this generation the widow will be saved. 'Her sons round your table are like olive shoots.'* And so shall the man be blessed 'who fears the Lord'.*

Ps 127:3
Ps 111:1

III

Lord, you are rich, and your store house never fails. Feed today this poor man with the crumbs that fall from the table of your children.* I am your beggar, crying at your door that I have had nothing to eat today. Lord, I am so feeble that I cannot open my mouth to speak. What strength he had who said: 'I opened my mouth and drew breath.'* Therefore, Lord, open my lips that I may be fed in praising you.* Your praise is true food. All your city of Jerusalem lives by no other food; for 'you fill it with the finest bread',* and 'you quench its thirst at the fountain of your delight'.* Alas for the men who go hungry for want of this praise. 'They sit upon the dunghill and drink the filthy water of their sins';* for they pant after the things of this world so that they may satisfy themselves with the sinful pleasures of the flesh. To such men as these your earth is like brass and your sky like iron: 'for three years and a half no rain has fallen'* because they yield no fruit, neither faith nor good works.* Their earth is like brass, for their voices sound like tinkling cymbals;* and their sky is like iron because their hearts are hard and un- yielding.* Of such men the Psalmist says: 'God said to the sinner, To what purpose do you recite my commandments, and repeat

Cf. Mk 7:28

Ps 118:131

Cf. Ps 50:17

Ps 147:14
Ps 35:9

Is 36:12

Cf. Lk 4:25
Cf. Ps 103:13

Cf. 1 Cor 13:1

Cf. Sir 3:27

Ps 49:16   the words of my promise to you?'*

Such men do not live by your praise, Lord:
they die of hunger, not for want of bread and
Cf. Mt 4:4   water, but of your word.* Yet 'you have no
Cf. Dan 13:53   desire to destroy the just man's soul'* by
famine; for in a time of drought you com-
manded the raven and the widow of Sarepta
Cf. 1 Kgs 17   to feed your servant Elias.* You feed those,
Lord, who feed you; and so it was that for the
widow who fed you, 'neither the bin of flour
1 Kgs 17:16   nor the crock of oil failed'.* The raven and
widow both fed you, the widow with her
griddlecake, the raven with the meat brought
in the evening. Now the raven stands for the
sinner; Zaccheus the tax gatherer is the
Cf. Lk 19:2-10   raven,* he who perched in the sycamore tree.
'Today I must eat in your house', the Scrip-
Lk 19:5   tures say.* And so today the raven feeds
Elias. How so? 'See, I give the half of my
Lk 19:8   possessions to the poor.'* And so he fed
Christ, and with Christ, the poor: or rather in
the poor he fed Christ. With what? With
fleshly things, that is, with the things of this
world. To abandon fleshly and worldly things
for Christ, this is to feed Christ. And he did
this in the evening, at twilight, when it may
truly be said: 'morning and evening make
Gen 1:5   one day.'*

First the raven brings food, then the
the widow, for the raven becomes the widow,
the raven changes into a dove, and utters her
moans. Why? Because she is a widow, because
her bridegroom is dead; he who cleanses her
from her sins, from the raven's blackness. Her
husband is dead, and so she gathers two sticks
in his memory, so that she can make for

herself and her son, that is her spirit, a last
morsel and then die with her bridegroom.*   *Cf. 1 Kgs 17:12*
But first Elias has to be fed, and with this
morsel of fresh dough* a little cake of bread   *Cf. 1 Cor 5:7*
must be baked on the coals. Christ asks the
first fruits of our works; he asks us not to savor fine foods, but to be content with humble
fare,* avoiding the 'Pharisee's leaven, which is   *Cf. Rom 12:16*
hypocrisy'.* This 'simple and humble   *Lk 12:1; Mt*
mind'† is the morsel of bread baked on the   *16:6*
coals which Christ asks from us.   †*Cf. Job 1:1*

Nor ought a good housewife to be without
a little oil, because 'God loves a cheerful
giver';* but the wheat and oil she has seems   *2 Cor 9:7*
little to her because 'she hungers and thirsts
for righteousness'.* 'I have nothing', your   *Mt 5:6*
servant says, 'except a fistful of wheat in my
bin and a little oil in the crock';* and a fist   *1 Kgs 17:12*
can hold very little. The wheat is the fine,
pure brightness of faith, the crock a humble
and prudent watchfulness, lest the wind of
pride 'crumbles such glory into dust'* and   *Ps 7:6*
scatter it. He who realizes that he possesses
only a little must guard it more carefully lest
he lose also this.

So the raven and the widow, Lord, feed
you in Sarepta in the land of Sidon, for the
accursed fig tree shriveled in the land of the
Jews.* So it will be that tax gatherers and   *Cf. Mk 11:12-14,*
harlots will enter the kingdom of heaven be-   *19-22*
fore Pharisees.* In the house of the Pharisee   *Mt 21:31*
you were seated by the door; in the house of
the woman who was a sinner, you were given
the place of honor.* Feed, Lord, this chick of   *Cf. Lk 7:36-46;*
the ravens, this son of sinners lamenting to   *Jn 12:1-3*
you: 'Though my father and my mother have

abandoned me,* you will never abandon those
who hope in you.'*

IV

'You have hardened our hearts, Lord, you have hardened our hearts, so that we shall not fear you.'* 'You have put a cloud between yourself and us, and our prayers cannot penetrate it.'* Take away our 'heart of stone', Lord, as you have promised, 'and gives us a heart of flesh so that you can send your Spirit among us.'* When your Spirit comes to us he will lay as our base and foundation that 'fear of the Lord which is the beginning of wisdom'.* Fear makes a heart steadfast, so that the house of the seven gifts of your glory which rests upon it may stand firm. You know, Lord, how troubled and unstable my heart is, like dust and the sands of the sea; so that whatever I strive to build up I seem rather to heap in ruins about my head. It is well said: 'Jerusalem has sinned, and so she has become unsteady;* she wanders in and out, and gossips on street corners, finding rest insufferable, unable to stay in her own home.'* How well this describes the folly of my senseless soul! What can I do? Return to your true husband and stop running after everyone who crosses your path. For this is why you have become so 'fickle and despicable, walking the streets as you do'.* Jerusalem sinned, she became a street walker. So go back to your true husband and say to

Is 63:17

Lam 3:44

Ez 36:26

Ps 110:10

Lam 1:8

Pr 7:11, 10

Jer 2:36

him 'Chasten my flesh with fear of you.'* And
he will say to you: 'Keep your tongue from
evil speech',* master your greed, strangle
your lechery, silence at their source all the
forbidden stirring of your body.

'All who belong to Christ, crucify their
flesh.'* But this is not enough; pagans have
done this, and men 'greedy for worthless
reputation'* and hypocrites do it. They crucify their flesh, but they receive no reward
from Christ. And this is because they have
not the fear of God. Chasten my flesh with
fear of you. Many have crucified their flesh,
not for fear of you, but out of vainglory. This
is not enough, then. Chasten with your fear
the lechery not only of the body but also of
the soul. Vainglory is the lechery of the soul.
'You destroy all those who have left you and
gone whoring.'* What does it matter whether
the impurity of the flesh or the lechery of the
soul is the cause of our destruction? And so
we must carry a cross, which will crucify not
only our flesh but our soul as well. The cross
of the flesh is our body's mortification. The
cross of the soul is the fear of God. The fear
of God chastens the soul, so that it does not
stray to right or left.*

There is a third cross of the spirit, which is
love. The Apostle says, 'I am nailed with
Christ to the Cross:* who will separate me
from the love of Christ?'* This was why the
blessed Andrew would not be taken down
from his cross. This cross is the love that gives
us a heart of flesh, a soft and tender heart. So
we see that this most gentle victim,* Christ,
was crucified because of His great love.

Marginalia:
Ps 118:120
Ps 33:14
Gal 5:24
Gal 5:26
Ps 72:27
Cf. Josh 1:7
Gal 2:19
Rom 8:35
Cf. Gen 18:7

Therefore, whoever attains to this third cross
passes through the cloud between him and
God and pours out his prayer in His very
presence.* And so for six days the cloud veiled   *Cf. Lam 3:44*
Moses on Mount Sinai. But on the seventh
day the Lord called to him from the midst of
the dark cloud. The Lord's glory appeared
like burning fire upon the top of the mountain in the sight of the children of Israel. And
Moses went into the midst of the cloud, and
climbed to the top of the mountain.* What   *Ex 24:15-18*
are we to understand by these six days during
which Moses was concealed by the cloud, except these six virtues by which he attained
to wisdom?* Only at the top of the mountain   *Cf. Is 11:2-3*
of wisdom does the burning fire of love give
us a sight of God's glory. And whatever is
below this seventh degree of wisdom is to be
considered as darkness and cloud. Let the first
cross, then, crucify the flesh through fear and
reverence and knowledge, so that lechery may
be chastised by fear, arrogance by reverence,
excess by knowledge. Let the second cross
win for the soul fortitude, counsel and understanding, so that by fortitude it may terrify
the devil, and guide by counsel its neighbor,
by understanding itself. The third cross
transcends all this, and gathered into the unity
of love may sleep in true peace and take
its rest.*   *Cf. Ps 4:9*

V

In the beginning, Lord, you laid the founda-
Cf. Gen 1:1 tions of heaven and earth;* that is, you
created angels and men. But after this brief
mention of heaven and the angels, the Scripture confines itself to man alone. 'The earth',
it says, 'was empty and void, and there was
Gen 1:2 darkness upon the face of the abyss.'* We see,
Lord, the great and marvelous structure of
the world; it has its impact on all our senses;
its beauty and vastness never cease to tell us
of your immense wisdom, power and goodness, incomprehensible and everlasting; and
though it is beyond the grasp of our every
human sense and expression, its purpose is to
Cf. Is 65:17, 66:22;
2 Pet 3:13 direct all our attention to that new heaven
and that new earth* which, as you tell us, you
are even now creating.

You say in your gospel that 'My Father has
Jn 5:17 never ceased working and I work with Him'.*
What else is this work but a new heaven and a
new earth? You are making an earth out of
Cf. Gen 1:6-10 the abyss, and a heaven out of earth.* The
abyss is the sinner, but when you make light
2 Cor 4:6 shine out of darkness* 'that they might
cast off the works of darkness and put on the
Rom 13:12 armor of light',* you show that you have
created a new heaven and a new earth. Indeed
I realize, Lord, that my mind is that earth,
waste and void until now; it is the darkness

upon the face of the abyss. It is waste because it is tossed about on the waters of disquiet; it wastes itself upon follies and fantasies, and is void of the fruits of good works. Or, as another translation has it, it is invisible and formless. In its confusion it is like some hideous and tangled chaos, ignorant of its end or its beginning or its proper nature; unless it believes that it was wondrously formed by the creator of all things, and that after this life it is destined either for hell because of its deserts, or for heaven because of its creator's mercy. Truly it is formless, because it does not conform itself to the grace of virtue and the glory of that divine image in whose likeness it was made.* So it is hidden in the abyss of its blindness, and its creator's face is hidden by the darkness of its fantasies.

Cf. Gen 1:26

This is the state of my soul, my God, this is the state of my soul: It is a land waste and void, it is invisible and formless, and there is darkness upon the face of the abyss. Yet even this abyss 'lends me its voice':* This abyss, deep and dark, calls to an abyss* which is far above it. The abyss of my mind cries out to you, Lord, who are beyond all that sense can perceive,* asking you to create out of me too a new heaven and a new earth.

Hab 3:10
Cf. Ps 41:8

Cf. Phil 4:7

David asked for this, and we ask for it with him: 'Create a clean heart in me, Lord, and renew a right spirit within me.'* He knew that he had already been created, but now he asked to be created afresh, a new heaven and new earth. 'We have heard with our ears and our fathers have told us of the work that was

Ps 50:12

Ps 43:2

worked in their days.'* It is because of this work that you say: 'My Father has never ceased working, and I work with Him.' 'You have formed their hearts, each one indivi-

Ps 32:15

dually',* you have created light in them and separated light from darkness, calling the

Cf. Gen 1:3-5

light 'day' and the darkness 'night'.* This is the work which you performed in their days: the patriarch Abraham and so many others acknowledged that they were full of these days, even as were those of whom the Apostle said: 'Once you were darkness, but now you

Eph 5:8

are light in the Lord.'*

Most wonderful Creator, if still you perform this work which you performed in ancient days, why do you not then work it in my soul, which is waste and void, darkness upon the face of the abyss? Say 'Let there be

Cf. Gen 1:3

light', and there will be light.* This is the work which you performed in Lazarus and in Paul. The face of Lazarus was bound in a

Jn 11:44

cloth,* for there was darkness upon the face of the abyss. But when Paul was baptized, this

Acts 9:18

darkness fell away from his eyes like scales,* so that he could see the glory of the Lord

2 Cor 3:18

with face unveiled.* Like the hearts of the Apostles when they slept through your agony, the eyes of my heart are covered with these scales, so that it cannot waken at your call:

Mt 26:43

'their eyes were heavy.'*

'But now the hour has come, Lord, for us

Rom 13:11

to rise from sleep,* for your trumpet sounds, again and again: Rise, you who sleep, rise up from among the dead, and Christ will give

*Eph 5:14
†Ps 17:29

you light.'* Lighten my darkness, Lord,† and say to my soul: 'Let there be light, and there was light.'

VI

The waters flowed away and separated from the waters on high; they flowed down to the depths of the earth* and were frozen by the north wind. The bitterest wind blew from the north and froze them, so that they could not flow and return to their source, so as to flow purer back again. Rise, north wind, and blow away from me, and let the mists and hail and the spirits of the storm* flee with you. Because of you the gentle south wind tarries. 'Depart, north wind, and south wind, come.'* Come from the noonday light and melt the ice of my soul, so that it may run again and rise again to whence it sprang; for now it has flowed down to a lake of filth and has become like mire. 'She who was bred in the purple is now coated in filth.'* Come, south wind, and blow and lift me up with your warm breath.

From the beginning of time you moved over the waters which are above the heavens, containing them by your extraordinary power lest they should flow away and mingle with those which are of no use to your household. At the peal of that thunder which is but your gentle voice, do not let my clouds break, for 'my soul has chosen to be held on high by you'.* Lift us up above the lower waters which lie below the firmament; bring us

Cf. Gen 1:7

Ps 148:8

Sg 4:16

Lam 4:5

Job 7:15

where we may hear the praises of God most high and understand what we sing in the psalm: 'The voice of the Lord is above the waters, the God of majesty, the Lord, has thundered out over many waters.'* Let our waters quake at the sound of your thunder so that they may be dissolved into mist and distilled by your heat; draw them up out of the reeking dung and preserve them in transparent purity; and let 'the light of your face, which has left its mark upon us'* be seen clearly in us. The waters which are above the heavens, Lord, are hardened with perpetual heat into an enduring crystal, so that they cannot flow down again, but radiate flashes of fire to each other as they are struck by the dart of the supreme sun. 'Holy, holy, holy, Lord God of hosts.'* It is your voice which has taught them to imitate this unutterable song. At its call living beings move,* and the wheel also which move with them,* for 'the voice of your thunder wheeled about the earth, so that your lightnings illumined it'.* 'The earth was moved and it trembled',* for 'your path is in the sea, and your ways in many waters.'*

Return, my soul, return to your source. Sigh for God, the living fount, constantly recalling the words, 'When shall I come and appear before the face of my God?'* Let your inward tears 'be your bread by day and by night'* and 'lest you be swallowed up by a more surpassing grief',* take comfort sometimes and say: 'Why are you sad, my soul, and why do you afflict me? Hope in God, for I will confess Him my comforter and my God.'*

Ps 28:3

Ps 4:7

Is 6:3

Cf. Ezek 1:19
Cf. Ezek 1:15

Ps 76:19
Ps 17:8

Ps 76:20

Ps 41:3

Ps 41:4
2 Cor 2:7

Ps 41:12, 42:5

Lord God of Abraham, hasten to me today,
I beg you, and be merciful to me, your abject
sinner. 'For the virgin to whom I shall say:
Give me drink,* and who will answer: Drink,
and I shall give water to your camels,* is she
whom the Lord my God prepared for His
son.'* And behold, Rebecca approached, 'a
virgin very beautiful, and unknown to him
who was to be her husband'.* Oh Virgin of
virgins, my Lady, whose matchless beauty
'even the angels long to look upon',* turn, I
implore, your virgin's eyes upon me, toiling
and parched of tongue, and deign to give me
only one drop from your water pot on your
fingertip.* I know, Lady, I know with what
inestimable love you regard any faithful servant of the great Father, for you give the
drink of your mercy not only to him who
asks but even to his camels. Truly, Lady, you
are that maiden, beautiful indeed, not only a
virgin but also unknown to man, unknown,
indeed, to that vilest of creatures, seducer of
minds, who, terrified by the Holy Spirit who
filled your heart with light, has always fled
away from you. 'You are all beautiful, and
there is in you no flaw.'* Most beautiful of
face, most perfect of body, most holy of
spirit, what above all shines out in you is that
you are most ready to help the wretched in
their needs. For you were the first to draw
water from the deepest well of mercy, and
you carry your vessel, full of grace, upon the
shoulders of your powerful understanding.

But what did that maiden do, she who prefigured you, Lady? 'At once', it says, 'she
says, 'she rested on her arm' the vessel from

Cf. Gen 24:14; Jn 4:7
Gen 24:14
Gen 24:44
Gen 24:16
1 Pet 1:12
Cf. Lk 16:24
Sg 4:7

Gen 24:18-19

her shoulder, and, not content to give only to
the man who asked of her, she said: 'I will give
drink also to your camels'.* That is, you give
drink from your vessel, most blessed one, to
me, camel, sinner that I am, humpbacked,
deformed, twisted. Truly you feel for us in
our miseries more than we can ask or hope or
think. You who are so infinitely high above
us, lower your vessel from your shoulder to
your arm, so humble, so pliable; and a 'whole

Is 60:6
Cf. Gen 24:32

host of camels will flock to you',* for you to
tame, wash,* water, feed and stable in your
Father's house. O lovely Virgin, most lovely
in your virginity, give drink also to me, I beg,
and make room tonight in your house for
me, for you say: 'The house has plenty of

Gen 24:25

room'.* This earth is too small for mortal
men, and so men contend: this is my land—
these are my streams—this is my wood; but in
your domain there is room in plenty for us to
stay. Behold, I am an outcast, to be devoured

Cf. Ezek 39:4

by beasts and birds;* and of all who are dear
to me there is no one who could console me,
except you who alone, under God, take
account of my struggles and grief. Mother of
mercy, bring me into your Father's house so
that I do not stand outside and shiver with the
frost and cold, to suffer the terrors of the
night. Lead me in and wash my feet, so that I

Pr 7:18; Sg 2:17,
4:6; 2 Pet 1:19

may lie down with your camels till the day
dawns and shadows vanish.* And lead us
again to Isaac your spouse, who ponders in

Cf. Gen 24:63

the meadow day and night,* waiting for you
to bring back to him his flocks, and 'camels

Cf. Gen 37:25;
1 Kgs 10:2

bearing spices'.* Truly you are she 'whom the
Lord prepared for the son of my master',

prepared, it says, by the Lord, to be mother and wife and sister. From among all women you were chosen, and chosen from the beginning, 'full of grace, the Lord is with you'.*   Lk 1:28
The Lord God, the Father, prepared you for the Lord God His Son, in order that you might prepare us for Him, when you deign to ride on the back of this camel, kneeling before you. Prepare Him, your Son, to receive us and to be merciful to us "when He rises up to strike the earth with His word, as with a rod."*   Is 11:4

VIII

Feed us, Lord, as you promised to the heirs
of our father Jacob, 'filling every living being
with blessing',* a spiritual blessing 'of the
dew of heaven and of the richness of the
earth',* 'with the abundance of your wheat
and wine and oil'.* The wheat is your flesh,
the wine your blood, the oil the Holy Spirit.
This is the blessing which has come down on
us like dew from heaven, this is the blessing
which has made our earth rich, that earth
which once was accursed because of Adam's
deed.* But Adam never sowed the seed of
this wheat in the ground. For this dew from
heaven 'falls like rain upon the fleece, like the
showers that moisten the earth'.* It fell upon
the Virgin like rain, upon the people like
showers. Lady full of grace, 'all the tribes of
the earth are blessed'* through the riches of
your womb. Grace descended upon you like
rain from the highest heaven, and showers of
that same grace drop down gently from you,
as from the eaves of a noble house which
overhangs all our land.

O 'house of ivory',* royal palace stoutly
built 'with cedar panels',* with widest pros-
pect; what riches are contained in you!
Truly, you are that 'great ivory throne' of
Solomon, 'of workmanship the like of which
was not found in any kingdom'. You are

Ps 144:16

Gen 27:28

Ps 4:8; Gen 27:28

Cf. Gen 3:17

Ps 71:6

Ps 71:17

1 Kgs 22:39

1 Kgs 6:18

'adorned with fine gold' of purest wisdom, and as well fashioned in your unspotted virginity as Solomon's throne.* You have mounted the six steps of the active life, and upon the seventh, the quiet of contemplation, you enthrone the king of peace. 'Upon the steps on either side there stand twelve lion cubs',* the prophets and apostles, the mighty fathers of both Testaments, supported by your merits, gazing up in wonderment, like little children, to the heights to which you have ascended. 'Who is she', they say, 'who goes before us like the rising dawn, lovely as the moon, glorious as the sun, terrible as an army in battle array?'* Moreover, 'the seat of the throne has two supporting arms',* for God 'with His left arm supports your head, and His right arm embraces you.'* 'And by the arms of the throne two lions stand',* Gabriel the archangel and John the evangelist, one assigned to your right hand, the other to your left, Gabriel, rightly called 'the might of God', and John 'the son of thunder'* because of his great lion's voice.

Oh great, oh wonderful, oh incomparable work of a king most wise! It is little enough, lady, that this earthly throne was surrounded by lions and their cubs who look upon you in awe: the whole court of heaven gazes aloft and wonders at you, consummation of all the works of God's hand.* You who are filled with grace, what is this which you bear in your bosom? It is the Lord,* and you say, 'I am His handmaiden'.* 'He who is mighty has made me great.'* Well may you wonder at me, for I am great, but it is He who made me great

Cf. 1 Kgs 10:18-20; 2 Ch 9:17-19

1 Kgs 10:20

Sg 6:9
1 Kgs 10:19

Sg 2:6
2 Ch 9:18

Mk 3:17

Cf. Ps 8:4

Cf. Jn 21:7
Lk 1:38
Lk 1:49

who is mighty. He is the Lord and I His handmaiden: He is the dew and I the earth whence
the wheat grows: He is the manna, I the vessel, out of which came the scarlet dye, made
from the worm.* 'I am a worm and no
man.'† For 'man is like the grass',* but this
man was wheat. This wheat grew from the
dew of heaven and from virgin soil. The earth
and the dew are great, but He who made them
is mighty. One grain of wheat was born of
me, and of the abundance of that wheat it is
said: 'But if it shall die, it will produce great
fruit';* and dying, it gave an abundance of
wine, rising again and ascending; and 'it
poured out oil'* which, the apostle says, 'it
pours out abundantly upon us'.* This is the
abundance of wheat and wine and oil which is
produced from the dew of heaven and the
richness of earth.* O you, earth's richness,
filled with grace: as the flesh fit for sacrifice
is separated from the carcase,* so you are
separated from the sinful mass of humanity,
you who are filled with grace, filled with
wheat, filled with wine, filled with oil, filled
and overflowing with every gift of the Holy
Spirit. 'The Lord is with you':* with you in
the inner room of your heart, with you in
the bridal chamber of your womb, remaining
with you, persisting in you, never leaving you.
'The Lord is with you'; but what does 'with
you' mean? It means that the Lord is one
with you in the nature which is to be raised
high above the angels. God dwells in His
angels but not with them; God dwells in you
and with you. God is seated above His
angels, 'seated above thrones',* 'seated above

*Cf. Ex 16:20;
Lev 14:4-5, 14:
49-52
†Ps 21:7
*Ps 102:15

Jn 12:25

Sg 1:2

Tit 3:6

Cf. Gen 27:28

Cf. Lev 3

Lk 1:28

Ps 9:5

the cherubim'* and seraphim;† He is seated
and He reigns in all of these, but in all the
kingdoms of the earth there is no work
like you, His great ivory throne.*

'You are blessed among women.'* The fullness of grace which you possess overflows
upon the earth and saturates it,* in showers
which make its fruits abound,* 'and all gen-
erations will call you blessed'.* You are
blessed among women. It is a poor thing to be
blessed above men, for it is 'women who give
birth in anguish',* 'men who eat their bread
by the sweat of their brow.'* You give birth
without anguish, you are fed without toiling,
and still it is little enough that you are more
blessed than the angels; for they are fed by
God, but they do not feed Him. But you,
blessed one, feed Him who feeds both you
and the angels. 'And blessed is the fruit of
your womb',* in whom women and men
and angels are blessed; and you are blessed
above them all, because 'many of His daugh-
ters have amassed riches, but you have ex-
celled them all'.* For God 'has anointed
with the oil of rejoicing' the fruit of your
womb 'before all your companions',* 'and
we all have received a share of His fullness',* but you have received more abundantly than us all.

You did well, lady, to ponder upon that
greeting, strange and wonderful and honor-
able, which gave you so to ponder,* for there
is no understanding enough to discover all its
meaning. It was sent down to you from Paradise, for our earth could never bear such
fruit. Ponder upon its nature, breathe in its

*Ps 98:1
†Dan 3:55

1 Kgs 10:26

Lk 1:28

Cf. Is 55:10
Ps 64:11
Lk 1:48

Cf. Gen 3:16
Cf. Gen 3:19

Lk 1:42

Pr 31:29

Heb 1:9;
cf. Ps 44:8

Jn 1:16

Cf. Lk 1:29

scent, taste its sweetness, this fruit plucked
from the tree of life. 'Eat of this and live

*Cf. Gen 2:9, 2:16-
17, 3:22.*
†Jn 11:26

forever.'* It is you who bore the fruit which
man must eat if he 'will live for ever'.† For see
who it was who proffered it to you: no ser-
pent, but an angel, no ugly, writhing snake
but Gabriel, upright and fair. 'Hail', he said,
'you who are filled with grace.' How sweetly
did you smell to the angel, 'perfumed treasure

*Is 39:2
†Cf. Ezek 28:13

house',* paradise of delights,† how sweet-
scented was your fertile field which the Lord

Cf. Gen 27:27

had blessed* and which smelled so sweetly to
Gabriel when he exclaimed, 'Hail, full of

*Lk 1:28
†Cf. Sg 1:11

grace.'* Already he saw at rest in you† the
king whom he worshiped as he said: 'The
Lord is with you', and he felt as if the

Cf. Gen 27:27

fragrance of that blessing* was permeating
the whole world when he went on to say:
'You are blessed among women'; and he perceived the immense reward which your son

Cf. Rom 8:17

would in the end bestow upon all his co-heirs*
when he ended: 'And blessed is the fruit
of your womb.'

IX

Hasten, O wretched man, hasten to where you will find life. I ask you, my soul, why are you wasting away with hunger and grief: is there no one to give you counsel?* *Cf. Is 40:13; Mic 4:9* Hasten, unhappy creature, to your queen. Today she holds her great feast, when she receives the Son of the most high God into her bridal chamber. Today her royal nuptials are being kept,* *Cf. Mt 22:2* her wine cellars are open, her store- houses are unlocked,* *Cf. Gen 41:56* and the hungry are filled.* *Cf. 1 Sam 2:5* Hasten, make speed before the doors are closed.* *Cf. Mt 25:10* Lady full of grace, see how empty is my soul. Your whole house, my lady, is full of wheat and wine and oil.* *Cf. Joel 2:19* Your son is a second Joseph, and you are His store, His cellars of measureless depth.* *Cf. Gen 45* So you did not permit the wine to fail at the marriage feast; you said to your son, our loving Jesus: 'They have no wine'.* *Jn 2:3* Knowing what wine you possessed, you counseled Him to give us drink; and truly, lady, had we not lacked our accustomed wine, you would not have prompted Him to give us His remedy. 'Our wine is dragons' gall';* *Deut 32:33* let this deadly cup pass from us,* *Cf. Mt 26:39* so that your life-giving drink be given to us and suffuse our being. Let our hearts rejoice in your wine and your song.* *Cf. Ps 103:15 Cf. Sir 9:15; Mt 26:29* Today is a royal marriage feast: Those whom you love drink the new wine* and sing

Cf. Ps 32:3
Ps 44:2

a new song.* There your psalmist David sings: 'My heart bursts forth in tuneful song'.* He had eaten and drunk, and now his heart burst forth in song. And where was this? In God's holy place, for the devout priest had given him that bread to eat which was to be eaten

Cf. 1 Sam 21:6

only by the priests.* He sings a new bridal song for the bridegroom and for the bride: 'the song of the feasting in a cry of exulta-

Ps 41:5

tion'.*

But how can a man sing who is gnawed by hunger? He has cause for mourning, not singing. It is I, lady, I who 'am dying of

Lk 15:17

hunger'.* Barely a trace of flour or oil

Cf. 1 Kgs 17:12

remains to me;* but your store of oil is

Cf. 2 Ch 32:38

filled* and running over, so that the jars of all the poor who look up to you can be filled. You abound in wine, in oil, in wheat, for you are that vast storehouse of Joseph your son in which the wheat of the seven

Cf. Gen 41:47-49

fertile years is laid up,* that wheat 'whose

Gen 41:5

every stalk grows seven richest ears'.* Our seven will be barren and mildewed, unless

Gen 41:6-7

'they can devour your fair wheat ears'.* Egypt would have perished to a man, had it not been saved by the abundance of your store. Come from afar, from the ends of the earth, come, you brothers of Joseph dying of hunger, come with your beasts of burden and your sacks, 'come and buy and eat'. Buy

Is 55:1

though you have no money,* and you will recognize Joseph; more than this: he will recognize you. He will remain a stranger to you, unless he can sit down among you and

Cf. Lk 24:30

break bread with you.* 'Serve them with

Gen 43:31

food',* he says.

The food is served separately to Joseph, and to the Egyptians, and to Joseph's brothers, 'for it is forbidden to the Egyptians to eat with Hebrews, and they would think such a feast ungodly.'* But why does Joseph eat apart? Because 'I have trodden the winepress alone, and from the nations no man is at my side'.* Eat then in the noonday,† eat, Joseph's brothers, and rejoice in your wine,* and you will recognize Joseph, for it says that after they had eaten at his table, 'he could no longer contain himself, but wept aloud, and even the Egyptians heard him',* for 'the noise of it went out over all the land'.* 'I am Joseph—is my father still alive*—does the old man still live?'* If he still lives, it is astonishing; yet he both lives and is dead, for he is our old man, Adam,* who, hearing the name of his son Joseph, comes to life again, and, 'as if waking from a dream',* says: 'It is enough for me to go and see him before I die.'* 'Bring him to me',† he says, 'put on the new man',* so that he may live, for the old Adam is dead.* 'It is now two years since famine first came to the land',* because 'the love of many men grows cold',* 'and still there are five more years' in which even our five talents will be lost.* 'A time is coming such as there has never been since first there were men';* 'and there will be plagues and famines'.* Joseph too has his poor to care for: 'he will fill the hungry with good things, and the rich he will send away empty.'*

Gen 43:32

Is 63:3
†*Cf. Sg 4:6*
Cf. Sg 5:1

Gen 45:1-2

Ps 18:5

Gen 45:3

Gen 43:27

Cf. Rom 6:6

Gen 45:26

Gen 45:28
†*Gen 44:21, 45:13*

Eph 4:24

Cf. Rom 6:6

Gen 45:6

Mt 24:12

Gen 45:6;
Cf. Mt 25

Dan 12:1

Mt 24:7

Lk 1:53

X

'He who eats my flesh and drinks my blood will have eternal life.'* Teach us, good master,* you who alone 'teach knowledge to man',* teach us how we ought to eat your flesh and to drink your blood. For we know, Lord, how your words 'are spirit and life';* but 'carnal man does not perceive those things which are of the Spirit of God';* because those who wished to understand these words by their own intellectual powers 'quarreled among themselves'* and so they did not 'draw honey out of the rock'.* Some even of your disciples broke their heads against this rock and left you* with the words: 'This is a hard saying.'* But it was you, Lord, who struck the rock, and there flowed out 'great plenty of water, so that the people and their beasts might drink'.* But it was the people alone who 'drank from that spiritual rock which journeyed with them',* for no beasts, because they are beasts, can drink of spiritual waters.

You have lowered the heavens and come down,* Lord, you have condescended to speak in our simple language; but then 'you make the cloud your chariot',* for it is by your flesh that you bring us to the Spirit. Your flesh is of no benefit to those who remain mere creatures of flesh,* but it does

Jn 6:55
Cf. Mk 10:17
Cf. Ps 93:10

Jn 6:64

1 Cor 2:14

Jn 6:53
Deut 32:13

Cf. Jn 6:67
Jn 6:61

Num 20:11

1 Cor 10:4

Cf. 2 Sam 22:10

Ps 103:3

Cf. Jn 6:64

benefit those who advance through flesh to
the spirit. We know, Lord, that we can truly
eat your flesh and drink your blood physi-
cally; but what we beg of you is that your
Spirit teach us how to eat your flesh and
drink your blood spiritually; since the spirit
can neither eat nor drink.

But let us too make the cloud our chariot
to the Spirit, let us cross over from the known
to the unknown, so that from the ways in
which the body eats and drinks, we may exam-
ine how the spirit also eats and drinks in its
own special way. For example, when we eat
earthly, tangible bread, first a fragment is
separated from the whole loaf and placed into
the mouth, and then when it has been broken
up by the teeth and moistened by the saliva
we swallow it; so that this food passes into
the stomach, and its strength and nourishment is distributed over the whole body.
Christ is truly the bread of the soul, 'the living
bread which came down from heaven',* feed- *Jn 6:41*
ing Christ's people, in faith now but in the
future life with the vision of Christ Himself.* *Cf. 2 Cor 5:7*
For it is by faith that Christ lives in you,* *Cf. Eph 3:17*
and faith in Christ is Christ in your heart. As
much as you believe in Christ so much do you
possess Him. And Christ is the same bread to
all who believe in Him, for there is only 'one
Lord, one faith',* even though some may *Eph 4:5*
receive the same gift of faith more fully,
others less fully. Nor are there as many faiths
as there are believers: for if it were so, each
faith would be controlled by its believer, and
not all believers by the faith. Now, as there is
only one truth, so one faith in one truth

governs and feeds all those who believe, and
it is one and the same Spirit who gives to
each of us as He wills.*

Cf. 1 Cor 12:11

Cf. 1 Cor 10:17

Therefore we all live by the same bread,*
each of us receiving his own share; and yet
each one of us has the whole of Christ, except
for those who break the bond of unity. When
I say 'the whole of Christ', I do not mean that
you can know as much of Christ as Christ
knows of Himself, for there is no angel in
heaven nor any creature who can do that. But
in this gift which I have received I possess the
whole of Christ and Christ possesses the
whole of me, just as the limb which is
possessed by the whole body in its turn
possesses the whole body. Therefore that portion of faith which has been distributed to
you is the fragment put in your mouth; but
unless you reflect, often and devoutly, on
what you believe, unless you will as it were
break it up into small pieces with your teeth,
that is, with your spiritual senses, chewing it
and turning it over in your mouth, it will
stick in your throat, that is, it will not go
down into your understanding. For how can
anything be understood which is thought
about only rarely and carelessly, especially
when it is something so subtle and invisible?
Faith offers to us those things which we cannot see, and there must be great intellectual
labor and toil before such things are passed
down into the mind. Unless this dry bread
be first moistened by the saliva of wisdom

Jm 1:17

Cf. Ps 126:1

coming down 'from the Father of light',*
you will labor in vain,* for what you have
gathered up by thinking does not penetrate

to your understanding. So the holy man Job said: 'Before I eat I sigh,'* and the bride in Canticles said: 'My soul has melted because my beloved has spoken.'* Therefore, your faith will be idle, unless by often thinking about it 'you can earn your bread by the labor of your hands'.* And yet you still cannot think at one and the same time about all that you believe, or understand at once all that you think, but only by degrees and as it were in fragments; and so your food can be properly prepared only by great labor.

For faith is in the memory as an invisible mother, who can only conceive when fructified by the dew of heaven, who cannot give birth to her son without great travail. This son is the word begotten of the understanding, in which faith itself can see itself best, reproduced in an image most like to itself. But understanding will never cease bringing this word to birth, until faith is wholly transformed into the sight of God; and then 'it will no longer remember its travail because of its joy that a man child is born into the world',* the child which before was enclosed in the womb and was brought forth by daylong labor and groaning. The soul which is sterile, which does not constantly give birth to this son, is accursed. Therefore let God's law be always on your lips* by constant meditation, so that you may always bring forth good understanding. It is by the understanding that this spiritual food is turned into love in the heart, so that what you understand you do not ignore, but cherish in love. You will have understood to no

Job 3:24

Sg 5:6

Ps 127:2

Jn 16:21

Cf. Ps 36:31

purpose unless you love what you understand,
for wisdom consists in love. For understanding goes before the spirit of wisdom, and
receives only a passing taste; but love savors
solid food. It is in love that all the strength of
the soul consists, it is into love that all life-
giving nourishment flows, it is from love that
life is poured into every limb and gives it
power; and Scripture says: 'Guard your heart
with every care, for it is thence that life
Pr 4:23   proceeds.'*

Love, therefore, is placed in the center of
the soul, like a man in the body, and these
three of which we have spoken, faith, meditation and understanding, grow and take full
shape to serve love's purpose, so that all subsequent qualities proceed from love and are
directed by it. First, imitation proceeds from
love; for who is there who would not wish to
imitate what he loves? Unless you love Christ
you will not imitate Him, that is, you will not
follow Him. For He said to Simon Peter after
Jn 21:19   He had tested his love: 'Follow me',* that is,
'Imitate me'. The feet of Judas may have
followed Christ, but what his heart followed
was avarice; and Gehazi followed Elisha not
Cf. 2 Kgs 5:20-27 out of love but cupidity.* But Christ must be
followed with the love of our whole heart.
So Meribbaal did not follow King David in
Cf. 2 Sam 19:25-26 time of trial, because he was lame:* yet
Christ must be followed at all times, but
most of all when we are afflicted, because it is
in difficulties that a friend is tested. Christ
*Lk 14:27;   says: 'Whoever does not carry his cross and
Mt 10:38   follow after me is not worthy of me.'* Simon
of Cyrene indeed carried the cross and

followed Christ,* but he did not share in the   *Cf. Lk 23:26*
torments of the cross. We must follow Christ
and we must cling to Him, and we must not
desert Him until death.* 'As the Lord lives',   *Cf. Phil 2:8*
Scripture says, 'and your soul lives, I shall
not leave you';* and Elisha never left his   *2 Kgs 2:2*
master until he was carried up in a chariot of
fire.* There were seventy-two disciples who   *2 Kgs 2:11*
followed Christ,* but when they had heard   *Lk 10:17*
Him say what they could not understand, they
turned back.* At the time of His Passion Peter   *Cf. Jn 6:67*
followed Him, but from afar, because he was
to deny Him.* There was only the thief who   *Cf. Mt 26:58*
followed Him to death upon the cross.*   *Cf. Mt 27:38*
Should I say that it was the thief who followed Christ to the death of the cross, or
Christ who followed the thief? Truly, Christ
followed the thief until the thief could flee
no farther, and when flight failed the thief,
he followed Christ, and with Christ entered
into Paradise.*   *Cf. Lk 23:43*

So, therefore, Christ must be followed, and
we must cling to Christ. 'It is good for me to
cling to God',* Scripture says, and 'my soul   *Ps 72:28*
has clung to you, and your right hand has
held me up'.* 'Whoever clings to God is one   *Ps 62:9*
spirit with Him':* not one body only, but   *1 Cor 6:17*
one spirit. The whole of Christ's body lives by
His spirit, and it is by His body that we come
to His spirit. Enter the body of Christ in faith,
and then you will be one spirit with Christ.
Now you are joined by faith to His body, and
afterward you will be joined to Him in spirit
by seeing Him. And just as here there is no
faith without the spirit, so there the spirit will
not be without the body, for our bodies

then will be not spirits but spiritualized. 'Father', Christ said, 'it is my wish that, as you and I are one, so these may be one in us,

Jn 17:21

so that the world may believe.'* This is union with God by faith; and a little later He said: 'So that they may be made perfectly one, and

Jn 17:23

the world may recognize it';* and this is union with God in the vision of Him.

This is what it means to eat the body of Christ spiritually: to have pure faith in Him, and carefully meditating upon that same faith, always to seek, and understanding what we seek, to find, and ardently to love what we find, and to imitate as much as we can what we love, and in imitating Christ, to cling to Him steadfastly, and clinging to Him, to be made one with Him for all eternity.

XI

Now let us go on to the chalice, for first Christ's flesh is eaten, and then His blood is drunk. It is for those who have been made perfect to accept this chalice of salvation, the chalice which Jesus drank, and they do this when their sufferings are acceptable to God. So in the eighth beatitude it is said: 'Blessed are those who suffer persecution for the sake of righteousness.'* The first seven beatitudes tell how Christ's body is eaten, the eighth how His blood is drunk. Food has to be chewed, and effort and time is needed before it is digested, but drink is quickly and easily swallowed; and in the same way moral discipline and the steady practice of virtue are only learned by time and effort, but the sufferings of the perfect are very sweet to them and seem to pass quickly by: 'how wonderful is your chalice, which brings me cheer'.* This good cheer, lovely and sweet, turns sorrow into delight, and to the perfect it does not seem that 'the sufferings of this time,' a time so short, 'are too small a price to pay for the glory of the time to come'.*

Is there anyone capable of savoring and understanding the Lord's mercies* who who would refuse the chalice of blessing from His hand, refuse to drink and share in His sufferings?* 'Taking the chalice', it says, 'He

Mt 5:10

Ps 22:5

Rom 8:18

Cf. Ps 106:43

Cf. Jer 25:17; 1 Cor 10:16

Mt 26:27
gave thanks.'* He who receives Christ's chalice must do more than receive it, he must also give thanks that he has been made worthy of such an honor as drinking from it. It was the

Cf. Ps 88:28; Col 1:15; Heb 1:6
first born and the prince of all creation* who first took it and drank from it and gave thanks, and then gave it to His disciples,

Mt 26:27
saying: 'Drink from this, all of you.'* He excluded no one; He wanted them all to share in His joy. First He took it and blessed it, and so the chalice of His suffering was consecrated. For if Christ's suffering, which was to bless our sufferings, had not preceded them, what would their use to us be? Our sufferings would then be not the blessing of sweetness but a cup of bitterness. It is the death of Christ which transforms the bitterness of our death into great sweetness. So, to those who are to drink Christ's blood, faith in His Passion is given, 'because Christ suffered for us, leaving

1 Pet 2:21
us an example'.*

But when we contemplate His blessed Passion, the re-presentation of this chalice of His, it excites a more burning thirst, which is our longing to bear His sufferings. So in the war of the Maccabees elephants were paraded, 'smeared with grape and mulberry juice to

1 Macc 6:34
look like blood, to incite them to battle'.* We thirst, and so we take the chalice, when our longing to suffer is turned into action. For who would drink unless he were thirsty? Christ Himself thirsted upon the cross when He drank. 'I thirst,' He said; 'but when they offered Him a sponge filled with vinegar, He

*Jn 19:28-29; Mt 27:34
would not drink when He had tasted it.'* Christ did not drink the vinegar of the old

malice* from the sponge which is an empty and deceitful heart, but wine from the pure, untainted cup of the new joy. Therefore, every man who drinks, that is, who suffers, should suffer not sadly but joyfully. So St. James says: 'Whatever kind of trial you encounter, my brothers, count it a great joy',* and the apostles 'left the presence of the council rejoicing, because they had been found worthy to suffer injuries for the name of Jesus.'* To glory in one's suffering: this is the meaning of 'drink and rejoice.' 'Eat, my friends', Scripture says, 'drink and rejoice, my dear ones.'* Those who eat together are counted friends, those who drink and rejoice together, dear to one another. But there are those who drink but do not rejoice, because in their afflictions they are not glad but sorrowful. 'Noah drank wine, and became drunk'* and fell asleep. Christ too at the time of His Passion fell asleep, for it is of Him that Scripture says: 'I have slumbered and slept';* and the bride in the Canticles too sleeps: 'I sleep', she says, 'and my heart is awake.'* Jacob slept upon his journey, while his heart kept watch and was astonished at the wonderful mysteries which he saw.* For what else is meant by sleeping than separating the mind from the bodily senses, so that it may keep watch in secret? So when the body sleeps let the heart keep watch.

For we must sleep and we must rest. No one can rest unless his heart keep watch. 'In true peace shall I sleep and take my rest',* the Psalmist says, and Christ said to His disciples: 'Sleep now and rest.'* Sleep from

Cf. 1 Cor 5:8

Jm 1:2

Acts 5:41

Sg 5:1

Gen 9:21

Ps 3:6

Sg 5:2

Cf. Gen 28:10-12

Ps 4:9

Mk 14:41

worldly affairs, rest in the inner places of
your heart. 'It is a Sabbath of rest, and on
that day you must mortify yourselves.'* What
does this mean: How can it be a Sabbath of
rest if we mortify ourselves? There is no rest
in mortification; but when the flesh is mortified the spirit rests, when the flesh is crucified
the mind keeps its Sabbath of rest. There are
two kinds of rest to be understood in this
Sabbath of rest: in one, we keep the Sabbath
of rest from the work of the senses; in the
other, we rejoice in the love of spiritual
things. 'Everyone who is not mortified upon
this day shall perish from among the people.'*
No one shall share Christ's glory unless he has
shared Christ's sufferings.* After the seventh
day, the Sabbath of rest, we come to the
eighth day of the Resurrection, the day in
which we shall find everlasting life, the day for
which we look as we eat Christ's flesh and
drink his blood. He says: 'Whoever eats my
flesh and drinks my blood shall have everlasting life.'* We are destined for it now, though
we have not yet received it. Whoever eats
this flesh and drinks this blood in the spirit
'shall not see death for ever'.* For the faithless, even though they may chew Christ's
body, do not eat it in the spirit, and so they
are already dead and dwell in living tombs.

But now let us briefly sum all this up. It is
by faith that the chalice is offered to us, by
the chalice that our thirst is excited, by thirst
that we hasten to drink it. What we drink
makes us glad, and gladdened we sleep, and
sleeping we rest, and resting we possess
everlasting life.

Lev 23:32, 23:27

Lev 23:29

Cf. 1 Pet 4:13

Jn 6:55

Cf. Jn 8:51

XII

Do not rain down upon us, Lord, those quails* which are our fleshly longings, which cannot fly higher than two cubits from the ground,* because they cannot reach up to the gifts of your Spirit. Do not rain down upon us 'flesh like dust',* 'because the flesh is dust and goes back to dust',* and it will drag down the glory of your image into the dust. 'Everything which enters the mouth goes into the belly and is voided out into the sewer.'* This is the end of every fleshly delight, 'and the winged birds are like the sand of the sea'.* The bird eats its fill and flutters its wings, but soon it turns back to sand: It takes its pleasure, it flies for a time, but soon it is transformed into the sand of the sea. Every delight of the flesh ends in bitterness. For a little while it lifts up the unhappy soul, but soon it is weighed down again and falls back to the sand. But your manna, Lord, is in small particles, 'like the coriander seed',* and it falls in the early morning like the dew, not, like the quails, in the evening;* and when it is pounded in the mortar it becomes pale and sweet, 'like bread mixed with oil'.* That is that 'bread of angels which man ate'.* Unbelievers still say 'Manhu—What is this?',* for they look upon your words as little* and lowly and to be despised;* and so they revert

Cf. Ex 16:13

Cf. Num 11:31

Ps 77:27
Gen 3:19

Mt 15:17

Ps 77:27

Num 11:7

Cf. Ex 16:13

Num 11:8
Ps 77:25
Ex 16:15
Cf. Ex 16:14
Cf. Jn 6:61

Cf. Ex 16:2-3;
Num 11:5-6

Wis 16:20

Num 11:32

Cf. Ex 16:21

Sg 5:6

Ps 125:4

Ps 62:6

Ps 127:2

Cf. Num 11:8
2 Cor 6:5

Cf. Deut 4:9

Ps 18:11, 118:103

to their longings for flesh in abundance, the fleshpots of Egypt,* because they do not know nor have they tasted the savor hidden within that manna which 'contains all sweetness and delight'.* They revert to the eating of flesh, and they dry it in the sun 'round about the camps'.* This is a wonderful thing, that one and the same sun should dry up flesh meat and liquefy the manna.* Flesh meat is dried up so that it can last the longer; the wicked last longer in order to fulfil their pleasures. Yet the manna which you gave melted as the sun grew hot, for 'my soul melted within me, as my beloved spoke'.*

O noonday sun, grow hot above us, so that the manna may melt and its fragrance may flow 'like the river in the south in flood'.* O children of Israel, gather it up, gather up the manna and pound it in the mortar, and 'your soul will be filled as with choice flesh and richness'.* It is a heavy labor, but its fruits are sweet. 'For you will feed from the labor of your hands', and then 'you will be blessed', and in the future 'it will be well with you'.* Pound, I tell you, your body and your soul in the mortar, and you will find what is best in them: pound* your body 'in fasts, in labors, in watchings',* your soul in the study of God's holy law. Never let His law be silent in your heart:* turn it round and about, look at it this way and that, and then you will understand how sweet the manna can taste. The psalmist did this, and he said: 'Lord, how sweet are your words in my mouth, sweeter than honey and the honeycomb.'* Like that wise virgin, the bee, gather manna from the

blossoms. You have 'a garden of delight',*   *Gen 3:23; Joel 2:3*
filled with roses and lilies, lovely in its won-
derful variety.* Whatever you will find there   *Cf. Est 1:6*
is sweet and fragrant: lay up in your basket an
abundant store of honey to be sweet to your
taste. What more shall I say? Honey to the
bee, the brook to the hart,* 'bread that   *Cf. Ps 41:2*
strengthens the heart of man',* it is all one   *Ps 103:15*
and the same food. This is that bread mixed
with oil which heals the sick, which strengthens the healthy, which 'rejoices the countenance';* and it contains every delight and   *Pr 15:13*
every sweet flavor.* Where are the quails,   *Cf. Wis 16:20*
where is the dried flesh? Truly, they rot in
the teeth of those who feed on them.* And   *Cf. Num 11:33*
if they rot in their teeth, how much more in
their bellies! And without doubt they rot,
like 'the beasts in their own dung'.* But that   *Joel 1:17*
bread of the angels which man ate can never
rot: It goes not down into the sewer but up to
the highest heaven, and it draws man up, back
to the place from which he received his
likeness.

CISTERCIAN PUBLICATIONS, INC.
TITLES LISTING

—CISTERCIAN TEXTS—

THE WORKS OF BERNARD OF CLAIRVAUX

Apologia to Abbot William
Five Books on Consideration: Advice to a Pope
Homilies in Praise of the Blessed Virgin Mary
The Life and Death of Saint Malachy the Irishman
Love without Measure: Extracts from the Writings of St Bernard (Paul Dimier)
On Grace and Free Choice
On Loving God (Analysis by Emero Stiegman)
The Parables of Saint Bernard (Michael Casey)
Sermons for the Summer Season
Sermons on Conversion
Sermons on the Song of Songs I–IV
The Steps of Humility and Pride

THE WORKS OF WILLIAM OF SAINT THIERRY

The Enigma of Faith
Exposition on the Epistle to the Romans
Exposition on the Song of Songs
The Golden Epistle
The Mirror of Faith
The Nature of Dignity of Love
On Contemplating God, Prayer & Meditations

THE WORKS OF AELRED OF RIEVAULX

Dialogue on the Soul
Liturgical Sermons, I
The Mirror of Charity
Spiritual Friendship
Treatises I: On Jesus at the Age of Twelve, Rule for a Recluse, The Pastoral Prayer
Walter Daniel: The Life of Aelred of Rievaulx

THE WORKS OF JOHN OF FORD

Sermons on the Final Verses of the Songs of Songs I–VII

THE WORKS OF GILBERT OF HOYLAND

Sermons on the Songs of Songs I–III
Treatises, Sermons and Epistles

OTHER EARLY CISTERCIAN WRITERS

The Letters of Adam of Perseigne I
Alan of Lille: The Art of Preaching
Baldwin of Ford: Spiritual Tractates I–II
Gertrud the Great of Helfta: Spiritual Exercises
Gertrud the Great of Helfta: The Herald of God's Loving-Kindness
Guerric of Igny: Liturgical Sermons I–[II]
Idung of Prüfening: Cistercians and Cluniacs: The Case of Cîteaux
Isaac of Stella: Sermons on the Christian Year, I–[II]
The Life of Beatrice of Nazareth
Serlo of Wilton & Serlo of Savigny: Works
Stephen of Lexington: Letters from Ireland
Stephen of Sawley: Treatises

—MONASTIC TEXTS—

EASTERN CHRISTIAN TRADITION

Besa: The Life of Shenoute
Cyril of Scythopolis: Lives of the Monks of Palestine
Dorotheos of Gaza: Discourses and Sayings
Evagrius Ponticus: Praktikos and Chapters on Prayer
Handmaids of the Lord: The Lives of Holy Women in Late Antiquity & the Early Middle Ages (Joan Petersen)
The Harlots of the Desert (Benedicta Ward)
John Moschos: The Spiritual Meadow
The Lives of the Desert Fathers
The Lives of Simeon Stylites (Robert Doran)
The Luminous Eye (Sebastian Brock)
Mena of Nikiou: Isaac of Alexandria & St Macrobius
Pachomian Koinonia I–III (Armand Veilleux)
Paphnutius: A Histories of the Monks of Upper Egypt
The Sayings of the Desert Fathers (Benedicta Ward)
Spiritual Direction in the Early Christian East (Irénée Hausherr)
Spiritually Beneficial Tales of Paul, Bishop of Monembasia (John Wortley)
Symeon the New Theologian: The Theological and Practical Treatises & The Three Theological Discourses (Paul McGuckin)
Theodoret of Cyrrhus: A History of the Monks of Syria
The Syriac Fathers on Prayer and the Spiritual Life (Sebastian Brock)

WESTERN CHRISTIAN TRADITION

Anselm of Canterbury: Letters I–III (Walter Fröhlich)
Bede: Commentary on the Acts of the Apostles
Bede: Commentary on the Seven Catholic Epistles

CISTERCIAN PUBLICATIONS, INC.
TITLES LISTING

Bede: Homilies on the Gospels III
The Celtic Monk (U. O Maidín)
Gregory the Great: Forty Gospel Homilies
The Meditations of Guigo I, Prior of the
Charterhouse (A. Gordon Mursell)
Peter of Celle: Selected Works
The Letters of Armand-Jean de Rancé I–II
The Rule of the Master
The Rule of Saint Augustine
The Wound of Love: A Carthusian Miscellany

CHRISTIAN SPIRITUALITY

Abba: Guides to Wholeness & Holiness East &
West
A Cloud of Witnesses: The Development of
Christian Doctrine (David N. Bell)
The Call of Wild Geese (Matthew Kelty)
Cistercian Way (André Louf)
The Contemplative Path
Drinking From the Hidden Fountain
(Thomas Spidlík)
Eros and Allegory: Medieval Exegesis of the
Song of Songs (Denys Turner)
Fathers Talking (Aelred Squire)
Friendship and Community (Brian McGuire)
From Cloister to Classroom
The Silent Herald of Unity: The Life of
Maria Gabrielle Sagheddu (Martha
Driscoll)
Life of St Mary Magdalene and of Her Sister
St Martha (David Mycoff)
Many Mansions (David N. Bell)
The Name of Jesus (Irénée Hausherr)
No Moment Too Small (Norvene Vest)
Penthos: The Doctrine of Compunction in the
Christian East (Irénée Hausherr)
Rancé and the Trappist Legacy
(A.J. Krailsheimer)
The Roots of the Modern Christian Tradition
Russian Mystics (Sergius Bolshakoff)
Sermons in A Monastery (Matthew Kelty)
The Spirituality of the Christian East
(Tomas Spidlík)
The Spirituality of the Medieval West
(André Vauchez)
Tuning In To Grace (André Louf)
Wholly Animals: A Book of Beastly Tales
(David N. Bell)

—MONASTIC STUDIES—

Community and Abbot in the Rule of St
Benedict I–II (Adalbert De Vogüé)
The Finances of the Cistercian Order in the
Fourteenth Century (Peter King)
Fountains Abbey & Its Benefactors
(Joan Wardrop)

The Hermit Monks of Grandmont
(Carole A. Hutchison)
In the Unity of the Holy Spirit (Sighard
Kleiner)
The Joy of Learning & the Love of God:
Essays in Honor of Jean Leclercq
Monastic Practices (Charles Cummings)
The Occupation of Celtic Sites in Ireland by
the Canons Regular of St Augustine and
the Cistercians (Geraldine Carville)
Reading Saint Benedict (Adalbert de Vogüé)
The Rule of St Benedict: A Doctrinal and
Spiritual Commentary (Adalbert de
Vogüé)
The Rule of St Benedict (Br. Pinocchio)
Serving God First (Sighard Kleiner)
St Hugh of Lincoln (David H. Farmer)
Stones Laid Before the Lord (Anselme Dimier)
What Nuns Read (David N. Bell)
With Greater Liberty: A Short History of
Christian Monasticism & Religious
Orders (Karl Frank)

—CISTERCIAN STUDIES—

Aelred of Rievaulx: A Study (Aelred Squire)
Athirst for God: Spiritual Desire in Bernard of
Clairvaux's Sermons on the Song of
Songs (Michael Casey)
Beatrice of Nazareth in Her Context
(Roger De Ganck)
Bernard of Clairvaux & the Cistercian Spirit
(Jean Leclercq)
Bernard of Clairvaux: Man, Monk, Mystic
(Michael Casey) Tapes and readings
Bernard of Clairvaux: Studies Presented to
Dom Jean Leclercq
Bernardus Magister (Nonacentenary)
Christ the Way: The Christology of Guerric of
Igny (John Morson)
Cistercian Sign Language (Robert Barakat)
The Cistercian Spirit
The Cistercians in Denmark (Brian McGuire)
The Cistercians in Scandinavia (James France)
A Difficult Saint (Brian McGuire)
The Eleventh-century Background of Cîteaux
(Bede K. Lackner)
A Gathering of Friends: Learning &
Spirituality in John of Forde (Costello
and Holdsworth)
Image and Likeness: The Augustinian
Spirituality of William of St Thierry
(David N. Bell)
An Index of Authors & Works in Cistercian
Libraries in Great Britain I (David N.
Bell)

CISTERCIAN PUBLICATIONS, INC.
TITLES LISTING

The Mystical Theology of St Bernard
(Etiénne Gilson)
Nicolas Cotheret's Annals of Citeaux (Louis J.
Lekai)
A Second Look at Saint Bernard (Jean
Leclercq)
The Spiritual Teachings of St Bernard of
Clairvaux (John R. Sommerfeldt)
Studiosorum Speculum (Louis J. Lekai)
Towards Unification with God
(Beatrice of Nazareth in Her Context, 2)
William, Abbot of St Thierry
Women and St Bernard of Clairvaux
(Jean Leclercq)

MEDIEVAL RELIGIOUS —WOMEN—

*Lillian Thomas Shank and John A. Nichols,
editors*
Distant Echoes
Peace Weavers
Hidden Springs: Cistercian Monastic Women
(2 volumes)

—CARTHUSIAN— TRADITION

The Call of Silent Love
Guigo II: The Ladder of Monks & Twelve
Meditations (Colledge & Walsh)
Interior Prayer (A Carthusian)
Meditations of Guigo II (A. Gorden Mursell)
The Way of Silent Love (A Carthusian
Miscellany)
The Wound of Love (A Carthusian Miscellany)
They Speak by Silences (A Carthusian)
Where Silence is Prayer (A Carthusian)

–STUDIES IN CISTERCIAN– ART & ARCHITECTURE

Meredith Parsons Lillich, editor
Volumes II, III and IV are now available

—THOMAS MERTON—

The Climate of Monastic Prayer (T. Merton)
The Legacy of Thomas Merton (P. Hart)
The Message of Thomas Merton (P. Hart)
The Monastic Journey of Thomas Merton
(P. Hart)
Thomas Merton Monk & Artist (Victor
Kramer)
Thomas Merton on St Bernard
Toward an Integrated Humanity
(M. Basil Pennington ed.)

CISTERCIAN LITURGICAL —DOCUMENTS SERIES—

Chrysogonus Waddell, ocso, editor
Hymn Collection of the Abbey of the Paraclete
Institutiones nostrae: The Paraclete Statutes
Molesme Summer-Season Breviary (4 volumes)
Old French Ordinary & Breviary of the Abbey
of the Paraclete: Text & Commentary
(2 volumes)
The Cadouin Breviary (2 volumes)
The Twelfth-century Cistercian Hymnal
(2 volumes)
The Twelfth-century Cistercian Psalter
The Twelfth-century Usages of the Cistercian
Lay brothers
Two Early *Libelli Missarum*

STUDIA PATRISTICA —XVIII—
Volumes 1, 2 and 3

❖ ❖ ❖ ❖ ❖ ❖ ❖ ❖ ❖ ❖ ❖ ❖ ❖

*Editorial queries & advance book
information should be directed to the
Editorial Offices:*

Cistercian Publications
Institute of Cistercian Studies
WMU Station
Kalamazoo, Michigan 49008
Tel: (616) 387-8920 ❖ Fax: (616) 387-8921

Cistercian Publications is a non-profit
corporation. Its publishing program is
restricted to monastic texts in translation
and books on the monastic tradition.

*North American customers may order these
books through booksellers or directly from the
warehouse, (address below):*

Cistercian Publications
St Joseph's Abbey
Spencer, Massachusetts 01562-1233
Tel: (508) 885-8730 ❖ Fax: (508) 885-4687

British & European Orders:

Cistercian Publications
Mount Saint Bernard Abbey
Coalville, Leicester LE67 5UL
Fax: [44] (1530) 81.46.08

❖ ❖ ❖ ❖ ❖ ❖ ❖ ❖ ❖ ❖ ❖ ❖ ❖

*A complete catalogue of texts in translation
and studies on early, medieval, and modern
monasticism is available, free of charge,
from Cistercian Publications.*